CW01192818

Gustav Mahler   Richard Strauss

Correspondence 1888–1911

GUSTAV MAHLER
RICHARD STRAUSS

Correspondence
1888–1911

edited with notes and an essay by
HERTA BLAUKOPF

translated by
EDMUND JEPHCOTT

faber and faber
LONDON BOSTON

First published in Germany in 1980 as
Gustav Mahler Richard Strauss Briefwechsel 1888–1911
by R. Piper & Co. Verlag, Munich
First published in Great Britain in 1984
by Faber and Faber Ltd
3 Queen Square London WC1
Filmset in Monophoto Ehrhardt
by Latimer Trend & Co Ltd Plymouth
Printed in Great Britain by
The Thetford Press Thetford Norfolk
All rights reserved

© *R. Piper & Co. Verlag, Munich, 1980*
Translation © *Faber and Faber, 1984*

British Library Cataloguing in Publication Data

Mahler, Gustav
Gustav Mahler–Richard Strauss
1. Strauss, Richard   2. Composers—Germany—Biography
3. Mahler, Gustav   4. Composer—Austria—Biography
I. Title   II. Strauss, Richard   III. Blaukopf, Herta
780'.92'4   ML410.S93
ISBN 0-571-13344-4

Contents

Foreword	*page*	11
Acknowledgements		13
Notes on the Edition		15
CORRESPONDENCE 1888–1911		17
RIVALRY AND FRIENDSHIP An Essay on the Mahler-Strauss Relationship *by Herta Blaukopf*		101
Key to Principal Bibliographical Sources		159
Notes		160
Chronologies: Mahler Conducts Strauss; Strauss Conducts Mahler *compiled by Knud Martner*		164
General Index		167
Index of Works by Mahler		171
Index of Works by Strauss		172

Illustrations

PLATES

between pages 96 and 97

1. Mahler waiting for Strauss, Salzburg, 1906 (*Internationale Gustav Mahler Gesellschaft, Vienna*)
2. Mahler, 1907 (*Internationale Gustav Mahler Gesellschaft, Vienna*)
3. Strauss, 1907 (*Österreichische Nationalbibliothek*)
4. Autograph MS page of *Feuersnot* (*Städtische Musikbibliothek, Munich*)
5. Autograph MS page of Mahler's Fourth Symphony (*Gesellschaft der Musikfreunde, Vienna*)
6. The Strauss Family (*Alice Strauss*)
7. Alma and Gustav Mahler, about 1903 (*Archiv der Wiener Philharmoniker*)
8. Announcement of Strauss's performance of Mahler's First Symphony, Buenos Aires, 1923 (*Archiv der Wiener Philharmoniker*)
9. Facsimile of Mahler's letter to Strauss, 19 August 1905 (*Strauss-Archiv*)
10. Facsimile of Strauss's letter to Mahler, June 1901 (*Alfred and Maria Rosé Collection, Ontario*)
11. Announcement of Mahler's performance of Strauss's *Symphonia domestica*, Vienna, 1904 (*Gesellschaft der Musikfreunde, Vienna*)

TEXT ILLUSTRATIONS

Fig. 1. Mahler, caricature and silhouette by Hans Schliessmann *page* 64
Fig. 2. Strauss, silhouette by Hans Schliessmann 137

Foreword

For almost a quarter of a century Gustav Mahler and Richard Strauss were linked by friendship. What joined them—and also what divided them—has a great deal to tell us about musical life from 1887 to 1911, in which both played a significant part not only as composers but as conductors and organizers.

Until now, without access to their correspondence, the nature of the relationship between the two composers has not been well understood. Although it was known that about sixty letters from Mahler to Strauss were in the Richard Strauss-Archiv at Garmisch-Partenkirchen, Strauss's letters to Mahler were scattered throughout the world. After a long search it has been possible to track down twenty-eight letters from Strauss to Mahler—in the original, or copies—from the most diverse places. Thus we have at last recovered enough of their extensive correspondence—representing perhaps three-fifths of the total—to merit publication. All the known letters are now published here.

These letters, together with existing material and with much new evidence unearthed by the Gustav Mahler Gesellschaft, have enabled me, in the essay which forms the second half of this book, to put into clearer perspective than before the 'rivalry and friendship' between Strauss and Mahler.

While this book was already in the press, a further written communication from Mahler to Strauss came to the editor's attention. This is an undated letter card which was written early in 1903. In it Mahler expresses his delight that Strauss has put his Second Symphony on the programme of the festival of the Allgemeiner Deutscher Musikverein (June 1903) in Basle. At the same time he declares that he is worried about the positioning of the chorus and orchestra, and most of all about the acoustics of the cathedral in Basle where the performance is to take place.

H.B.   Vienna, October 1983

Acknowledgements

The Internationale Gustav Mahler Gesellschaft, under whose auspices this book was prepared, would particularly like to thank Dr Franz Strauss and Frau Alice Strauss of Garmisch-Partenkirchen who, as custodians of Mahler's letters, gave much vital information and advice. Without the generous co-operation of Dr Franz Strauss, who sadly did not live to see the book appear, the letters could not have been published.

Our thanks are likewise due to Frau Anna Mahler of Spoleto for her valuable guidance, and to the many other people and institutions who have supplied copies of original letters, or other information. These are listed in alphabetical order below:

Bayerische Staatsbibliothek, Munich
Gottfried von Einem, Vienna
Professor Marius Flothuis, Amsterdam
Gemeentemuseum, The Hague
Frau Maria Feuer, Budapest
Haus-, Hof- und Staatsarchiv, Vienna
Professor Franz Grasberger, Vienna
Internationales Opernarchiv, Clemens M. Gruber, Vienna
Frau Alena Kersovan, Hamburg
Henry-Louis de La Grange, Paris
The Gustav Mahler/Alfred Rosé Room, The Music Library, University of Western Ontario, London, Ontario
Professor Eduard Reeser, Bilthoven
Lyman W. Riley, Assistant Director of Libraries for Special Collections, Alma Mahler-Werfel Bequest, The Charles Patterson Van Pelt Library CH, University of Pennsylvania, Philadelphia
Ernest Rosé, Washington DC
Maria Rosé, London, Ontario

Acknowledgements

Professor Marcel Rubin, Vienna
Dr Willi Schuh, Zurich
Staatsarchiv, Leipzig
Professor Rudolph Stephan, Berlin
Professor Jonathan Sternberg, Philadelphia
Frau Eleonore Vondenhoff, Frankfurt

The present collection must not be regarded as final. Further letters and documents may well come to light from both public and private collections. At the Internationale Gustav Mahler Gesellschaft—the centre for research and documentation on Mahler—we are always glad to receive information about any such material.

While this book was already in the press, a further written communication from Mahler to Strauss came to the editor's attention. This is an undated postcard which was written early in 1903. In it Mahler expresses his delight that Strauss has put his Second Symphony on the programme of the German music societies' festival (June 1903) in Basle. At the same time he declares that he is worried about the positioning of the chorus and orchestra, and most of all about the acoustics of the cathedral in Basle where the performance is to take place.

H.B.

Notes on the Edition

If no other source is given for the Mahler letters, the text is based on the autographs in the Richard Strauss-Archiv. For the few letters that come from other collections, as for the letters from Strauss, the source is given in each case.

The layout of dates, numbers, addresses, salutations and valedictions has been standardized. Underlining—very frequent in Mahler's letters—has been represented, as is usual, by italics, while all titles have been italicized, whether the authors remembered to underline each one or not.

In the case of the twelve letters and postcards from Strauss which have survived only in a typed transcript by Alma Mahler (now in the Alma Mahler-Werfel Bequest, University of Pennsylvania) the text reproduced here naturally follows that typescript.

Unlike Strauss, whose letters are dated almost without exception, Mahler sent off most of his letters undated, and with only a fragment of his own address, at best. Like all editors of Mahler's letters, I therefore faced a number of difficult dating problems. Sometimes it was possible to determine the exact date on which a letter was written, sometimes only an approximate one could be given. Doubtful cases are discussed in footnotes. Dates supplied by the editor are given in square brackets, as are all other editorial additions.

H.B.

PUBLISHERS' NOTE

The publishers would particularly like to thank Knud Martner, Copenhagen, for his help in preparing the English edition of this book.

The extracts quoted in Herta Blaukopf's essay (pp. 103–58) from previously published letters by Mahler have been newly translated, although, to help the reader locate the complete letters, the sources cited in the Notes (pp. 160–3) are the familiar English-language editions detailed on p. 159.

CORRESPONDENCE
1888–1911

Mahler to Strauss

Hotel Blauer Stern
Prague
[August 1888][1]

Dear Colleague

Since my return to Munich is likely to be seriously delayed, would you be kind enough to let me know what steps I should take in order to have a symphony of mine[2] performed in the next concert season in Munich—and whether there is any prospect of this.

No doubt Levy [sic] is not yet in Munich,[3] and it seems high time for works to be submitted.

Please, dear friend, give me a little advice and—help, if it is possible.

With sincere regards
Gustav Mahler

---

[1] Mahler spent part of the summer of 1888 in Munich, then travelled to Prague where he rehearsed and conducted his adaptation of Weber's *Die drei Pintos* at the German Theatre in Prague.

[2] Mahler's First Symphony, completed in March 1888.

[3] Hermann Levi (1839–1900), Court conductor in Munich. Richard Strauss's 'Grey Diary', 5, p. 12, contains the following recollection, possibly going back to 1888: 'At Levi's I also got to know Mahler's First Symphony, with a very original, humorous funeral march that we immediately played four-handed from the score.'

Correspondence 1888–1911

Mahler to Strauss

The Director
Royal Hungarian Opera
Budapest
[January 1891][1]

Dear Friend

Permit me an inquiry in confidence. I have engaged Herr Grützmacher,[2] whose contract you were kind enough to undersign as a witness, as solo cellist—under the impression that he was the Weimar cellist known to me.[3] But I see from the papers that this is a *third* Grützmacher[4] of whom I know nothing except that he departed *suddenly* from Sondershausen.—Could you please let me know *very confidentially* whether you know Herr G. as a musician and what is your opinion of him.

At the last Philharmonic concert here I had the pleasure of hearing your tone poem *Aus Italien* for the first time,[5] and found the last two movements particularly delightful. The effect on the audience was, unfortunately, not as powerful as I should have wished, as the organizers had the incomprehensible idea of putting your composition at the end of an over-long concert.

I should very much like to hear more from you—(I mean, personally, as well) and secretly hope that you may tell me a little about yourself in your reply.—

With kind regards
Yours sincerely
Gustav Mahler

---

[1] Second half of January 1891. *Aus Italien* was played for the first time in Budapest at the Philharmonic concert on 14 January.

[2] One of a family of German cellists whose most important member was Friedrich Grützmacher (1832–1903).

[3] Leopold Grützmacher (1835–1900), conductor of the Weimar Court Orchestra.

[4] Friedrich Grützmacher jun. (1866–1919), Leopold's son, who began his career at the Court Orchestra in Sondershausen.

[5] Symphonic fantasia, Op. 16, first performed in 1887 under Strauss in Munich.

Correspondence 1888–1911

Mahler to Strauss

[October 1891][1]

Dear Friend

I shall, I promise you, do everything in my power to put on the two Ritter operas here,[2] and to instil true life into them by the most careful possible production. Pollini,[3] however, (who is away at present) not only holds *power* here but unfortunately *wields* it to the full, so that I can vouch only for *myself*, and not for any undertaking by us both. But as soon as he is back from his travels I shall take the matter in hand.—That you are now doing *Tristan* gives me sincere pleasure, both for you and *Tristan*. How fine to be able to build a work up from the foundations.

I pushed it through here last month *without* cuts (ditto the *Meistersinger*). They were Pyrrhic victories, however—in Pollini's eyes, at any rate, my standing was lowered.—Now good luck with your *Tristan* 'without tempo changes'!

My 'scores',[4] dear friend, I am now consigning to my desk. You do not know what *incessant* rebuffs I receive with them. To see over and over again how the gentlemen one approaches are overcome by consternation, declaring it an *impossible* audacity to perform such things—this finally grows unbearable.—This endless, fruitless peddling.

A week ago Bülow[5] almost gave up the ghost while I was playing from them to him.

You have not gone through anything like that and cannot understand that one begins to lose faith.

Good heavens, world history will go on without my compositions.

With warmest regards
Yours sincerely
Gustav Mahler

Could I not have a look at your *Don Juan* and *Tod und Verklärung*?[6]

---

[1] On 7 September 1891 Mahler, Principal Conductor at the Hamburg Stadttheater since the end of March 1891, put on a production of *Tristan und Isolde* that: 'apart from the opening of the great duet in Act II', was without cuts (*Hamburger Fremdenblatt*, 8 September 1891).

[2] *Der faule Hans* (first performance 1885 in Munich) and *Wem die Krone?* (première 1890 under Strauss in Weimar) by Alexander Ritter (1833–96).

[3] Bernhard Pollini (1838–97), Director of the Hamburg Stadttheater.

Correspondence 1888–1911

[4] At this time probably only *Das klagende Lied*, the First Symphony and *Totenfeier* (see p. 111).

[5] Hans von Bülow (1830–94), conductor and composer living in Hamburg since 1887.

[6] Tone poems by Strauss. *Don Juan*, Op. 20, was first performed in 1889 in Weimar, *Tod und Verklärung*, Op. 24, in 1890 in Eisenach at the Festival of the Allgemeiner Deutscher Musikverein.

Mahler to Strauss

[24 January 1892][1]

Dear Friend

I received the enclosed letter a few weeks ago from my 19-year-old brother in Vienna.[2] I have come across it again by chance, and it occurs to me that it might interest you to know what an impression your *Don Juan* has made on young people in Vienna.[3] —

I hope you found the scribble of the critics there as amusing as I did. — I have heard much praise of your *Tristan* and congratulate you sincerely on it.

With cordial regards
Gustav Mahler

[1] The date is written, unlike the letter, in pencil, possibly not by Mahler although it is approximately correct.

[2] Otto Mahler (1873–95), at that time studying music in Vienna.

[3] *Don Juan* was performed at the Philharmonic concert on 10 January 1892 under Hans Richter. On 31 January 1892 Strauss wrote to his father: 'The success in Vienna seems to have been partial: yesterday, Mahler (Hamburg) sent me a letter from his 19-year-old brother in Vienna who writes about the work very enthusiastically, in depth and with great understanding. The young have been won over!' (*RST Eltern*, p. 148, see key to abbreviations on p. 159.)

Correspondence 1888–1911

Mahler to Strauss

Fröbelstrasse 14 III
Hamburg[1]
[20 October 1893][2]

My dear Friend

On Friday the 27th of this month I am conducting a concert in Hamburg in which a number of my own compositions will be performed.[3] (I am the only living conductor who is interested in my compositions, and am therefore taking the first opportunity that presents itself.)—

It would be a great pleasure to me if you would do me the honour of being present.—From the newspapers I see that you are well again and in Weimar.[4] Hamburg is not too far away. Please let me know whether you are able and willing to come.

With what interest I look forward to your 'opera', you can imagine.[5]— Would it be quite impossible to hear or see something from it?

Looking forward to hearing from you soon,

Very sincerely yours
Gustav Mahler

---

[1] As far as we know, this was Mahler's first private address in Hamburg—he had stayed at first at the Hotel Streit. From Fröbelstrasse 14 he moved to Parkallee 12, and finally to Bismarckstrasse 86. The dates of the moves are not known.
[2] An approximate date confirmed by Strauss's reply, see below.
[3] Mahler performed six songs from *Des Knaben Wunderhorn*, and the First Symphony in the revised version of 1893 with the title 'Titan'.
[4] Strauss had been seriously ill in 1892, and in November went to recuperate in the Mediterranean and in Egypt. He returned in the summer of 1893.
[5] Strauss's first stage work *Guntram*, on the text and score of which he worked from 1887 to 1893.

Strauss to Mahler

Weimar
22 October 1893

My dear Friend[1]

It is unfortunately quite impossible for me to accept your kind invitation. I should have been delighted to come, but on 27th and 28th I have to conduct *Lohengrin* rehearsals and cannot get away.

Correspondence 1888–1911

I thank you most warmly for thinking of me—but that you are the only living conductor interested in your compositions is simply not true: when I asked you two years ago to send me something from your symphonies you turned me down; don't you remember?

Germany I can no longer abide, climate and artistic conditions are too miserable! In Egypt the sun shone constantly, and of theatre 'not even a trace'!

My *Guntram* is to come out in Munich at the beginning of February; at the moment all is at the copyist's!

With best wishes for a fine success on Friday,

Yours very sincerely
Richard Strauss

[1] Autograph in the Bayerische Staatsbibliothek, Munich.

Mahler to Strauss

Fröbelstrasse 14 III
Hamburg
24 December 1893

Dear Friend

When is your 'opera' to be put on in Munich? Or are there difficulties?—I surmise as much from the news now in the papers that the première is to take place in Karlsruhe.[1] In any case I should like to remind you that a musician understanding and standing by you (let us say for a change) is sitting here in Hamburg who would at all times count it an honour and a pleasure to smooth your path as far as his feeble powers allow.—

In a word—if a first performance should not come off anywhere else (thanks to the tender care of our lords intendants and directors—and perhaps even conductors), and if the Hamburg Stadttheater does not strike you as too unsuited, I am always ready to help remove such obstacles.

That the study and casting of the work would be done with the utmost devotion, I personally guarantee.

Sincerely yours
G. Mahler

[1] The Munich Opera had given no firm commitment and in December 1893 *Guntram* was accepted for first performance in Karlsruhe, although this première too failed to materialize.

Correspondence 1888–1911

Mahler to Strauss

[January 1894][1]

Dear Friend

Warmest thanks for sending me your text,[2] which has heightened my interest and suspense still more.—How will it all *sound*?!—I should be very grateful to you if, on your coming visit to Hamburg, you could let me hear some extracts from the work.

I count on spending much time with you, and put myself entirely at your disposal. Can I help you in any other way? Please, make use of me!

When will you arrive, and *where* are you going to stay?

If I am not held up, I should like to meet you at the station.

I look forward to seeing you again soon,

Yours
Gustav Mahler

[1] On 22 January 1894 Strauss conducted the seventh Hamburg Subscription Concert in place of Bülow, who was ill.
[2] The libretto of *Guntram*.

Mahler to Strauss

26 January 1894

Dear Friend

Thank you for your news.—I am extremely sorry that I cannot be with you on Monday,[1] as the *Bartered Bride* is being performed here.—Schuch got the fright of his life when he heard he had *you* as his immediate successor. Most probably it would 'detract' from him.[2]

It is *splendid* that you are *coming back!*[3] *Let me know when you arrive.* Would you prefer *not* to stay in a *hotel?* In that case a comfortable room would be prepared for you here with me.—

The 'Strauss case' has caused much turbulence in the usually placid waters of our local public. I could not help laughing at the different faces that it has brought to the fore.—Yesterday at a social gathering I gave somewhat short shrift to a famous musical dandy—a lesson of which various people will take note.

Correspondence 1888–1911

For a change I have read the reviews. Pfohl's gave me much pleasure.[4]

rings in the ear.[5]

Sacred G major! I am already busy smoothing the way.

Faithfully yours
Gustav Mahler

[1] 29 January 1894, when Strauss conducted the seventh Philharmonic concert in Berlin.
[2] Ernst von Schuch (1846–1914), conductor of the Court Opera and Court Orchestra in Dresden, conducted the sixth Philharmonic concert. In the following season (1894–5) all the Berlin Philharmonic concerts were entrusted to Strauss.
[3] Strauss was to conduct in Hamburg on 26 February 1894, but declined after a disagreement over the programme (see note, p. 32).
[4] Ferdinand Pfohl (1862–1949), critic of the *Hamburger Nachrichten*.
[5] Opening of the first Prelude to *Guntram*, in G major. Mahler does not quote it accurately.

Mahler to Strauss

27 January 1894

Dear Friend

You have probably received my letter by now.

As I wrote to you, I unfortunately have to conduct the *Bartered Bride* on Monday and cannot be with you. Please do not forget to send me your scores (at least the three tone poems).[1] Have you received the reviews from here? You must have had a good laugh over them![2]—Now everyone is crying: 'Guelph' and 'Ghibelline'![3]

I look forward immensely to our next meeting here in February.

With sincere regards
Gustav Mahler

[1] *Don Juan*, *Tod und Verklärung* and *Macbeth*.
[2] The symphonic fantasia *Aus Italien* that Strauss had presented on 22 January in Hamburg caused a storm of controversy.
[3] The allusion is to the struggle between the Welf and Staufer houses in medieval Germany [trans.].

Correspondence 1888–1911

Mahler to Strauss

Hamburg
2 February 1894

Dear Friend

Your news concerning Herr von Bronsart[1] makes me very happy—and I thank you most sincerely for your friendship.—I wrote to you twice in Berlin—to judge by your postcards you have not received the letters.—

I also addressed a question to you—whether you would not prefer to stay here, where a room would be prepared for you in accordance with your wishes. Please let me have your answer in good time.—On 13 February I have *Siegfried*—no luck again, I'm afraid! But I *must* go to Karlsruhe, come what may.

Only please send me, if it is at all possible, a vocal score for Birrenkoven,[2] so that I can prepare him a little for you in Bayreuth.

In any case we shall see each other here! I have a great desire to enjoy your *Guntram* again. Please bring it with you. This time, too, I shall be on the alert as 'conductor', though I am willing to bet that I could recreate the spirit of your works even without discussion with you. All the same, it gives greater security to know the author's wishes.—And do you know that your motifs pursue me in my dreams? I received a very enduring impression. I only notice this now that my first excitement over the work has died down. I look forward immensely to the time of the performance here, and to seeing you again in Hamburg. Do let me know when you arrive.—The Behns return your greetings most cordially.[3]

In sincere friendship
Yours
Gustav Mahler

Your offer to conduct my 'Titan'[4] I accept *most gratefully*, should I be prevented.

---

[1] Hans Bronsart von Schellenberg (1830–1913), Manager of the Court Theatre in Weimar, and from 1888, President of the Allgemeiner Deutscher Musikverein (founded in 1859 by Franz Liszt). Strauss had asked Bronsart to perform Mahler's First Symphony at the thirtieth Festival of the Musikverein which took place in June 1894 at Weimar.

[2] The tenor Willy Birrenkoven (1865–1955), who had been at the Hamburg Stadttheater since autumn 1893 and was engaged to sing Parsifal at the 1894

Bayreuth Festival. Mahler studied the part with him to help Strauss who was acting as répétiteur at Bayreuth.

[3] Dr Hermann Behn (1859–1927), a Hamburg lawyer and composer, a friend of Mahler's.

[4] The title of Mahler's First Symphony, added in 1893.

Mahler to Strauss

[3 February 1894][1]

Dear Friend

I am quite dumbfounded by your news.[2]—Only a few days ago Pollini asked when I wished to sign my contract. He remains extremely polite towards me.—I am therefore *quite unable* to form a judgement on this matter.—Pollini is up to all sorts of tricks. Heaven knows what he means to achieve by them.—In any case I ask you, dear Friend, to consider *only your interests*, just as in this case I shall think *only of mine*. This is undoubtedly the best course, since we would otherwise lose all power to direct events in dealing with such people.

As soon as I hear *anything*, however *slight*, I shall write to you. Should you be involved and your interests affected, I should telegraph if necessary.

I expect you have received the letter I sent yesterday. Behn told me yesterday that you had agreed to stay at his house; this of course cancels my invitation, since it is best for you to accept Behn's.

You will feel very much at home there.

Looking forward to seeing you soon,

Faithfully yours
Gustav Mahler

[1] It seems clear that this letter must have been written, as was the following one, on 3 February, the 'letter sent yesterday' being, presumably, that of 2 February.

[2] Strauss had told Mahler he was negotiating for an appointment at the Hamburg Stadttheater (see p. 114 f.).

Correspondence 1888–1911

Mahler to Strauss

Hamburg
3 February 1894
Evening

Dear Friend

Your news has plunged me into a state of considerable agitation, and the best thing would be to clear the matter up at once by confronting Pollini directly.—However, I should not wish to do so without your consent.

As the whole business can finally be only one of the *chess-moves* Pollini is so fond of, intended to dislodge me from my superior present position *vis-à-vis* himself, it can only benefit you to see matters clearly, and so I propose speaking to Pollini quite openly about it.

I beg you to let me know by return what you think of my proposal.—It goes without saying that I should drop it if you raised the slightest objection.

Yours very sincerely
Gustav Mahler

Mahler to Strauss

6 February 1894

Dearest Friend

I no longer know where I am! The day before yesterday Pollini came up to me during a performance and said in a jocularly blunt way: 'I'm fed up with waiting. Come to my office tomorrow so that we can get our contract straight at last!' I gave him a nonplussed look and said nothing. To be honest, I had already prepared myself for my departure. (In such matters I am somewhat fatalistic[1] and believe everything that happens to be for the best.)—

The next morning (that is, yesterday) as I came into the theatre, *Wolff*, who is in charge of the office, came up to me with a contract already signed by *Pollini* and accepting *all my demands*.

Today I intend to sign my side of the contract.—

I can therefore only think that Pollini wants *us both*, which is like him in that he is often overcome, incomprehensibly, by the most idealistic impulses.—You can imagine *how* delighted I should be! I know of no one with whom I feel such affinities, and in face of whom all petty promptings in me would be stilled. I should with the greatest pleasure relinquish the *Nibelungen* to you, and all else can be settled most amicably between us.—

I suggest, to set things in motion, that you simply accept (naturally without letting them know what I have written to you).—Otherwise he will really finish by appointing the 'famous' Grossmann.[2]

But at all events you should make sure of Berlin from '97 on; for I think that would be a marvellous field for you.[3]

My contract now runs for *five years*. But where are *Don Juan, Tod und Verklärung* and *Macbeth*?

Please send them to me very soon! I have already sent my symphony to Bronsart! How do things stand there regarding it?

In sincere friendship
Yours
Gustav Mahler

[1] Mahler was not really fatalistic. On the contrary, he had an almost morbid fear of being without a post.

[2] It is not clear who Mahler means. Joseph Grossmann was conductor at Budapest at the time, while Paul Grossmann was conductor at Posen.

[3] Strauss was hoping to become Felix von Weingartner's successor as conductor of the Berlin Opera.

Mahler to Strauss

Hamburg
26 February 1894

Dear Friend

Bülow's body should reach here in the middle of next month, arrangements for a memorial service are under way; I hope you will have time to be present.—I am ordering the wreath immediately.[1]—

Concerning *Guntram, I saw this coming.*—I have *known for four weeks* that *Guntram*'s position in Karlsruhe was precarious;[2] and I can tell you today that it will not be performed there for the time being.—I ask you to keep this confidential. When we next meet I shall name my source. Given the conception of your work, its uncompromising demands, I warn you in advance of the thorny path it will have to tread across our beloved 'German artistic institutions'. It will meet with the greatest difficulties from the theatre directors and the artistic personnel. I can already hear the catchwords: 'unperformable', 'voice-ruining', etc.

On me you can count *absolutely*; I shall personally champion the work no matter where I am, and *guarantee* you a performance prepared with utmost devotion.—Here the situation is as follows: Birrenkoven has to prepare *Siegfried* for us and *Parsifal* for Bayreuth, and we can hardly expect him to master *Guntram* at the same time. His talent and seriousness are beyond doubt; but his *intelligence* leaves something to be desired (between ourselves).—*April* is no time for a performance at a theatre that closes in *May*, and does so with a *Wagner cycle* that absorbs all the strength of the artists and all the interest of the public.—Also, I should need *time* to get not only the performance accepted by *Pollini*, but the necessary space and seriousness for rehearsals.—These are my reservations about an *April première* here.—However, should you think differently, or need one in any case for extraneous reasons, I shall exert all my influence to have your intentions met.—But I cannot promise I should be successful; nor do I believe I could achieve a performance matching the significance of the work.

My suggestion is this: procure the *earliest* possible decision in Karlsruhe, and then decide at once *for Hamburg*.—I shall do everything to produce the work here in late October or early November. You should send me the vocal score straight away and I shall do the preliminary study before the summer.—In Bayreuth you would put the final touches to Birrenkoven yourself.—The whole thing could then be discussed in every detail when you come here either for Bülow's funeral or whenever you would like to.—At any rate, please let me *know at once* what you think.—Pollini is not here at present but returns in the next few days; I shall speak to him *immediately*. But in the interests of the matter I must present it as if it is *not you* who wish for a first performance here, but that *I* wish to request this honour of you, and that you will grant it almost out of friendship to me.—Of the difficulties in Karlsruhe Pollini must know *nothing*, as he is dreadfully suspicious.—Concerning the *parts*, please permit me a word as a friend.—If I were to propose to Pollini a payment of 1,000 marks, it would give rise to difficulties and formalities out of proportion to so trivial a matter.—I have such a sum lying here quite superfluously. Allow me to offer it to you to pay the copyist.—Prove your friendship for me by simply saying 'yes', without wasting another word on the subject. The royalties for the work are, of course, agreed from the outset. I write this in great haste, to let you have an answer by return. I have not even a decent sheet of paper and therefore use the other half of your letter. This evening we have this tiresome 'Memorial

Subscription Concert',[3] which is quite odious to me. I am down as conductor, despite my protestations, but am only conducting the final piece: 'Eroica'! The female hysteria[4] that is putting forth the most unbelievable blooms here makes me think again and again *how very* right you were in *your* standpoint. Well—enough of that!

Let me soon have your word of command, and accept my sincere regards.

Yours
Gustav Mahler

People like us should never make concessions!

[1] Hans von Bülow had died on 12 February 1894 in Cairo.
[2] The singer of the title role did not feel equal to this difficult part.
[3] The ninth Hamburg Subscription Concert of 26 February 1894, that was to have been conducted by Strauss. When Strauss heard the news of Bülow's death, he changed his original programme and proposed Bülow's 'Nirwana', and works by Wagner and Liszt. In deference to the Hamburg Bülow community that was orientated towards Johannes Brahms and, furthermore, could not forgive Liszt's daughter Cosima for leaving her husband Bülow and marrying Wagner, this proposal was rejected. Strauss in his turn refused to conduct a work by Brahms. The concert was conducted by Mahler and Julius Spengel.
[4] In letters to his sister Justine, too, Mahler wrote scathingly of the cult of the dead Bülow kept up by society women.

Mahler to Strauss

Hamburg
24 March 1894

Dear Friend

Your letter reached me as I was describing to you—in a somewhat depressed frame of mind—the course taken by my efforts on behalf of *Guntram*.—As I had not yet approached Pollini with a request of this kind, I imagined things would be easier.—Naïve as I am, I expected that, if I go to Pollini and say, 'There is a man who is one of the hopes of musical Germany (and not only for hotheads, but is regarded without question as such by old and young)—he has composed an opera the text and music of which I know, and which I regard as the most significant dramatic achievement (and perhaps the only significant one) since Wagner's *Parsifal*. Do you want to put this work on? You will not incur costs of any kind.'—if I say this, then Pollini will say, 'Of course! Let me have it at once!' To my amazement Pollini has so far rejected the idea.

Now I am, of course, very far from conceding defeat, and I do not doubt that I shall finally get the work performed—as a last resort I can, on my side, always raise the 'question of confidence'.

But to achieve this by force would be mistaken, because I need the *time* and *goodwill* of all those concerned. If Pollini were to take it on against his will, as he will do soon, for example, with *Hiarne*,[1] he will simply 'throw' the thing on to the stage to be rid of it; and with your *Guntram* this is out of the question.

I must therefore 'hollow the stone drop by drop'. For this I need time.— It would be very important to *prepare the part* with Birrenkoven in the meantime. For all kinds of reasons that I will explain to you on your coming visit to Hamburg.

You can also achieve much with Pollini personally.—We will use your visit to strike while the iron is hot. And I will make sure the forge is heated up ready for your arrival.

So, at all events: I *shall have my way*—for I do not give in. Once I catch Pollini in a good mood (particularly at a moment when he needs a favour from me) all will go well. (I know this from experience.) For this reason I did not really want to write to you yet, for you would not believe how embittering this is to me. But on the other hand you *must* know about it; and finally, you too are used to 'waiting'—even if not so used as I am.

I am *extraordinarily* pleased about Munich for you,[2] although I would rather have seen you appointed at Berlin.—But that probably will happen too.

But be *sure* to come to Bülow's funeral service;[3] it is *very important* for *your opera*! Can I not have at least a vocal score of it? I must have this to interest Birrenkoven, and to have him sing something from it for *Pollini*. Experience has proved this a good method in such cases, since his vanity is flattered.—When is *Guntram* due in Weimar?[4] I hope *to be there for it*!

Yours most sincerely
Gustav Mahler

---

[1] An opera by Ingeborg von Bronsart (1840–1913), wife of the Weimar director. The only Hamburg performance took place on 17 March 1897 under R. Krzyzanowsky.

[2] On 20 March Strauss had signed a contract with the Munich Opera.

[3] The funeral took place on 29 March 1894 in Hamburg. Strauss did not attend the ceremony.
[4] The first performance took place on 10 May 1894.

Mahler to Strauss

1 May 1894

Dear Friend

I have answered [should read: waited] till today to answer your kind invitation[1] because I had first to know our repertoire for May. As I foresaw, the Wagner cycle and its rehearsals come at exactly this time, so that my presence is indispensable.—I must therefore forgo attending the first performance, much as I should have wished to, but hope to be there on 1 June [deleted: May].[2]

I have again broached the matter with Pollini, always with the same result.—However, I have another plan. Next winter I am conducting the Wolff concerts here,[3] as you will know.—In one of them I am doing the great scene in Act II, and before that the Prelude, with [deleted: *Guntram*] Birrenkoven, if you allow me.

However, time will bring the solution.—I think of you now in full spate, and am often with you in thought.—I regret very much that the vocal score you sent is so sketchy that often I should scarcely be able to make anything out if I had not heard it from you.

With Birrenkoven I am now zealously studying *Parsifal* and taking a real pleasure in that capital fellow.—

With cordial regards, and best wishes for your '*supreme* moment' (10 May).[4]

Yours sincerely
Gustav Mahler

I hope to see you on 1 July.

[1] To the first performance of *Guntram* on 10 May in Weimar.
[2] For the performance of *Guntram* at the Festival of the Allgemeiner Deutscher Musikverein.
[3] Hermann Wolff (1845–1902) was the owner of the H. Wolff Concert Bureau, which organized the Hamburg Subscription Concerts, previously directed by Bülow.
[4] The première of *Guntram*.

Correspondence 1888–1911

Mahler to Strauss

Fröbelstrasse 14
15 May 1894

Dear Friend

So *Guntram* has seen the light of day, and has thereby been given to the world in the fullest sense. On the unexpectedly happy outcome I congratulate not you but *us*. I cannot tell you how much I desire to hear it. I have been regretting more and more that I have only this short score, which even lacks all the orchestral interludes, and which, given such a special kind of composition, makes any true understanding impossible. I am only happy to have been prepared beforehand by yourself—and have drawn on those memories during these days.

Bronsart[1] writes that you will be so kind as to prepare my symphony.[2] I shall send you the parts tomorrow.—In addition I shall bring two copies of each of the string parts, which are at present being written out here; for the rehearsals in Weimar six 1st violins, five 2nd violins, four violas, four cellos and four double basses should be enough.—One other thing: the manuscript now in your hands no longer coincides in detail with the material I am sending. This has been considerably retouched to match the second copy which I now have, as I have taken advantage of the experience of the performance here. [27 October 1893]—Altogether, everything is more slender and transparent.—Will the original, unrevised score be sufficient for your preparations? Or should I send you my copy at once? I should have done this immediately in any case, were I not so afraid to think of the work entirely out of my hands and journeying about at the mercy of the post.—If you would nevertheless prefer it, let me know by return and I shall send it at once.—

I do have one request: please rehearse the winds and strings separately; I was forced to do so here as well.—I arrive in Weimar on the *29th*! When do I have my rehearsals?

Would you be so kind as to reserve me a room there somewhere, and a place at the performances for my brother, who would like to hear them. (It is the same young man whose letter I sent you earlier).—

Is it really true, as Herr von Bronsart wrote, that the string section has only ten 1st and eight 2nd violins? *That would be very hard*, for I really don't know how it would sound then! Can *nothing* be done to make up the numbers? I would take over part of the cost with pleasure.

I would also mention that the material is *entirely free of errors*, and in case of doubt should be given *precedence over* the *original* score.—

The instrumentation of the Introduction has been entirely changed for the strings, and the *scheme* for this is in the folder of music I am sending you.

Please let me hear about youself. *When is* Guntram *to be printed?* Best regards, till we meet in Weimar,

Yours sincerely
Gustav Mahler

[1] See note p. 27.
[2] Mahler's First Symphony, in D major ('Titan').

Mahler to Strauss

17 May 1894

Dear Friend

So be it: I am sending you the score as well.[1] Because of a collation that has become necessary I can only send off the material tomorrow! I am sending the score in a separate parcel.—

Your news concerning *Guntram* is really extremely surprising to me. So we have a repetition of the old story that is ever new. 'Naboth's vineyard is also here.' It changes nothing; your work will go on here next winter, if I have to resort to the basest means (courting Pollini, etc.).

This matters to me, among other reasons, because you will nowhere at this time find a more suitable casting for the title role than Birrenkoven, who is developing in a quite unsuspected manner in the *Parsifal* rehearsals. He will give you much enjoyment at Bayreuth.

Until now I have not had a chance to go through *Guntram* with him—the poor wretch is working too hard, and with the utmost exertion I can hardly find enough hours for *Parsifal* myself; it is too important at present.—At any rate I hope before leaving here to play the piece through for him, and no doubt you will go into it thoroughly with him at Bayreuth.—I'll give him his solo part to take with him.—Shall I also give him the short score or can I keep it with me.—I nibble at it daily, and am slowly piecing it all together.

How it will be built up in the orchestra—I'm in suspense to know! No doubt I shall have to keep my eyes and ears open. From your letter you seem rather depressed.—Dear Friend, that really isn't necessary!

'When dogs bark we see that we are riding', says Goethe! And you cut a fine figure on horseback! I look forward immensely to meeting you again. I hope you will be able to spare me a few hours!

Most sincerely yours
Gustav Mahler

I have told Birrenkoven a lot about *Guntram* and he is straining at the leash!

[1] Clearly the second copy mentioned in the previous letter that agreed with the new orchestral parts.

Mahler to Strauss

Steinbach am Attersee[1]
19 July 1894

Dear Friend

I am only now managing to answer your kind letter—you probably also find that the less you have to do, the less time you have. I am honest enough to mention this as my only excuse.—

How can you even ask whether I take your candour amiss? Believe me, I would not do so even if you clothed your criticism in a far less flattering garment.—

In the matter itself I cannot be of one mind with you; that you wish to find the conclusion and, as it were, a summary of the whole piece at the point you refer to merely shows me that I have not expressed myself at all *clearly*, which certainly would be bad enough. If it does not bore you, I shall come back to this at Bayreuth and explain my thoughts.[2]—Just one thing today: at the place in question the conclusion is merely apparent (in the full sense of a 'false conclusion'), and a change and breaking-down that reaches to the essence is needed before a true 'victory' can be won after such a struggle.

My intention was to show a struggle in which victory is furthest from the protagonist just when he believes it closest.—This is the nature of every *spiritual* struggle.—For there it is by no means so simple to become or to be a hero.—

Even if in later years (that is, when I had become *detached* from the matter) I became convinced that I had not succeeded in putting my truest intention into sound, I should not change anything. And do you know why? You will know it at once, if you ask yourself what you would do yourself in such a case: make *something new*, and the *whole* better! Am I not right—on that we agree?!

And now, after all, I will give you a valid excuse for my negligence: in these weeks I have finished the last movement of my Second Symphony. When you hear it you will understand that I had now to do other things than improving the skin I have shed: a new one that fits better has grown. Indeed, my new work is to the one you know as a man to an infant.

There are, after all, *seven years* between them—that means something at our age.—I hope to be in Bayreuth in the last days of this month, and hope to be more intensively with you than at the Weimar revels!

Most sincerely yours
Gustav Mahler

[1] Mahler's summer residence 1893–6.
[2] Mahler is replying to criticisms of his First Symphony in a letter from Strauss—now apparently lost (see p. 118).

Mahler to Strauss

[4 January 1895][1]

Dear Friend

The full score and vocal score of *Iphigenia* are now in my possession.[2] *P.*[3] has promised me to accept your version.—I have not yet discussed the conditions set by the publisher![4] I fear there will be difficulties, as the publisher is not *very fair* in this. I know P. too well in such matters! When the time comes (it is due out in *April*) I shall need your mediation. It's damnable that we are always having to be involved in such shabby affairs.

The parts *are ready* (for *my symphony*)[5] and in the next week I shall go through them with my orchestra!

Sincerely
Gustav Mahler

[1] The Hamburg postmark of this postcard which Mahler sent to Strauss in Munich where he had started his second engagement in the autumn of 1894.
[2] C. W. Gluck's *Iphigenia in Tauris*, arranged by Strauss in 1890 and published in 1895. Mahler never in fact performed Strauss's arrangement of this opera.
[3] Bernhard Pollini.
[4] Adolph Fürstner, Berlin.
[5] The first three movements of Mahler's Second Symphony.

Correspondence 1888–1911

Mahler to Strauss

Parkallee 12
27 January 1895

Dear Friend

The parts for the three movements of my symphony are ready, and already played.—It is *faultless*, and very *clear*, and strangely, *much easier* than my First Symphony.—

Where *shall I send it*? When is the *first* rehearsal?[1]

I would be glad to relieve you of *this* rehearsal, if you wish, and do the 'rough work' for you ...

In the next Subscription concert here the two Preludes to *Guntram* are being presented,[2] and at a *matinée* at the *Stadttheater* not long after Birrenkoven is singing your Grail narrative.[3]—In this way, I hope, we shall slowly set things in motion. I have not yet had a reply to my postcard (concerning *Iphigenia*). Please write by return, if only a card.

With best regards to you and your wife[4]
Yours sincerely
Gustav Mahler

---

[1] Strauss conducted the 1894–5 season of Philharmonic Concerts in Berlin, and included the first three movements of Mahler's Second Symphony in the programme of the ninth concert on 4 March 1895, which Mahler himself conducted.

[2] Mahler conducted the 1894–5 Hamburg Subscription Concert season, and included the Prelude to Act I of *Guntram* in the programme on 4 February 1895. The second Prelude was not in fact performed (see Mahler's next letter).

[3] The 'Friedenserzählung' aria from *Guntram*. The matinée did not take place (see Mahler's letter of 8 June 1895).

[4] On 10 September 1894 Strauss had married his former pupil, the singer Pauline de Ahna.

Mahler to Strauss

[5 February 1895][1]

Dear Friend

I should like to be in Berlin for the first rehearsal—or possibly take it off your hands entirely.—Please let me know [deleted: definitely] whether it is absolutely certain to take place on 18 February.—I need a lot of extra instruments for it, and ask you to be *absolutely sure* to provide these. I shall gladly *bear the cost myself*, as I know that this is not agreeable to Wolff.[2]

That is, *one E-flat clarinet*
one 2nd timpanist with *three timpani*
one 2nd harp

and at least *eight double basses*, of which, if possible, *one* or *two* should have a *C string*. For the percussion I need, apart from the two timpanists, three further people. That *six horns, four trumpets, four trombones, one bass tuba, one double bassoon, English horn, one bass clarinet* are needed, you will know from the score.—

One other thing: *could I have an extra rehearsal with the whole orchestra at my expense*, and *when?*
Please answer the above very soon!

When I come to Berlin I should like to go to Fürstner[3] *with you*, to settle the commercial side of *Iphigenia*. For this I am getting Pollini's authority. In March the *opera is to come out* (early April at the latest).

Yesterday I played your Prelude from *Guntram* (through Wolff's negligence—or incomprehension—only the one to *Act I*, although I had asked for both). I was *very* pleased with the performance, and still more with the audience, who were much affected. It sounded wonderful!

At the matinée I am now doing the Prelude to *Act II* before the great scene with Guntram. But it would have done no harm for the audience to have already heard it at the concert.—

Shall I send any reviews? (I never read them, to avoid irritation, as I have some very mean-minded opponents.)—

Please answer quickly!

Ever yours
Gustav Mahler

The German stage is behaving *disgracefully* towards your *Guntram*—and I should *not* have believed it *possible!*[4]

---

[1] Though undated, this letter was clearly written the day after the concert with the Prelude from *Guntram*, which took place on 4 February 1895.
[2] Hermann Wolff, concert artists' agent, was organizer of the Berlin Philharmonic Concerts as well as the Hamburg Subscription Concerts, see p. 42.
[3] The publisher Adolph Fürstner, see p. 38.
[4] Mahler is referring to the great difficulty Strauss had in getting any German Opera house to put on *Guntram*.

Correspondence 1888–1911

Mahler to Strauss

[6 February 1895][1]

Dear Friend

I have read the reviews after all, and am sending them to you just as they are. — I am glad, actually, that the rabble are behaving on the whole so decently. — Did you notice that almost all of them express the desire for a performance of the *whole work*? — This does not seem to have been lost on Pollini, for he asked about it today. —

Now comes my second blow — the great scene from Act II, and I hope my mine will go off. —

The only ass is, as ever, Herr Sittard.[2] I'm sending him too for the sake of completeness. — But most pleasing of all was the audience, who were very moved, if a little taken aback.

I say, and always will:

Best regards
Yours sincerely
Mahler

I have just noticed that I have not the *Fremdenblatt* to hand. Krause[4] reviews your Prelude *very favourably*, and demands the performance [of the whole work].

---

[1] See the following letter.
[2] Josef Sittard (1846–1903), critic of the *Hamburgischer Correspondent* and leader of the Hamburg musical conservatives.
[3] From Leonore's aria in Act I of Beethoven's *Fidelio*. The text is: '... far as it is, love shall attain it ...'. Mahler does not quote exactly.
[4] Emil Krause (1840–1916), critic of the *Hamburger Fremdenblatt*.

Correspondence 1888–1911

Mahler to Strauss

Parkallee 12 III
7 February 1895

Here, dear Friend, is the last review I promised yesterday.—The most important thing is that they all declare themselves in favour of a performance of the whole work.

Pollini is very dependent on such things.—Our 'stock is very high!' Now the second thrust, and we are at the desired goal. Please let me know if you have received what I have written yesterday and today.—

Finally, one more big request. It is very important to me to be present at the *first* rehearsal. On 18 *February* I *cannot* get away. Please give me a different day, and above all, if possible, a *special rehearsal* at *my expense*! Best of all, in the last week before the concert.—I don't know how things are arranged in Berlin, or to whom I should apply.—If it could be done without involving Wolff, I should prefer it.—Please do this for me as a friend; I am bringing the parts with me to the rehearsal. In haste,

Yours most sincerely
Gust. Mahler

Please write at once!

Mahler to Strauss

Steinbach am Attersee
8 June 1895

Dear Friend

Your letter reached me at my summer palace, where I have been for a few days. The reason why I have not written to you is simply and solely that I have had nothing to write. The *matinée* did not take place; I have in the meantime fallen out completely with Pollini, and tendered my resignation a few weeks ago.[1] So far it has not been accepted—my request has not even been answered.—What the reason for this may be I have not yet been able to divine.

Either Pollini will not let me go under any circumstances, and therefore breaks off any discussion of the matter; or he is secretly looking for a successor and will only reply when he has or has not found one.—That is why all my efforts to secure your work its deserved publicity have so far been confined to the sphere of pious hopes.—Be that as it may, whether I remain at Hamburg or soon find another sphere of activity, you know that I will do everything that lies within my power to attain this end. My gratitude to you, if nothing else, would oblige me to do so. You are really the only one of *all* my colleagues who has taken notice of my productions so far, (and will, I hope, continue to do so).—

How splendid that a new 'symph. poem' has arrived![2] How do you find the time? You are, to be sure, the most productive of us all. I was a little surprised at the title, as I knew that you wanted to treat the subject dramatically![3] What is the connection?—

At the end of August I am passing through Munich (or Bavaria); I shall not forgo visiting you if you are anywhere in the region! You will let me know, won't you, where I can meet you?

My sisters[4] return your kind regards. So Weingartner[5] is staying after all, we read? Well—now Berlin can sleep in peace again!

Most sincerely yours
Gustav Mahler

Best regards to your wife.
Please don't overlook my present address.

---

[1] Mahler stayed at the Hamburg Stadttheater until April 1897.
[2] Strauss's Op. 26, *Till Eulenspiegels lustige Streiche*, completed on 6 May 1895.
[3] Strauss had originally planned an opera entitled *Till Eulenspiegel bei den Schildbürgern* and had started working on the text.
[4] Justine (1868–1938) and Emma Mahler (1875–1933), at that time living with Mahler.
[5] Felix von Weingartner (1863–1942), conductor and composer, Court Conductor in Berlin since 1891, and from the autumn of 1895 also conductor of the Hamburg Subscription Concerts.

Mahler to Strauss

Hotel zum Askanischen Hof
Königgrätzer Strasse 21
Berlin W.
[December 1895][1]

Dear Friend

Although you are sure to know that on 13 Dec. a performance of my work[2] is taking place here, I cannot help announcing it to you especially, and expressing the heartfelt wish that I may see you here on that occasion.

You know what a pleasure it would be for me, and also that there is no one in the world I would rather have in my audience. — If you can, please come, dear Friend! May I say again: the three movements you know are only the *exposition* of the wòrk, and I think you might really like to hear the last one.

Yours very sincerely
Gustav Mahler

My kindest regards to your wife.

---

[1] Hermann Behn wrote to Strauss on 7 December 1895: 'It would be very good if you could be here on 13 December. I understand Mahler has invited you ...'

[2] Mahler's Second Symphony. The first three movements had first been performed on 4 March 1895 (see pp. 38–40, 42; at the concert on 13 December the whole symphony was played.

Strauss to Mahler

Herr Kapellmeister Gustav Mahler
Hotel Askanischer Hof
Königgrätzerstrasse 21
Berlin W.
[10 December 1895][1]

Dear Friend

Unfortunately, I cannot come, or do anything for you at the *N. Nachrichten*.[2] M. behaved so offensively over *Guntram* that I can have nothing further to do with him or his newspaper.[3] The best thing would be for you or Dr Behn, to whom please give my best regards, to contact H. Porges[4] who is responsible for the music reviews in the N.N. With best wishes for a glorious success,

In haste!

> Yours
> Richard Strauss

---

[1] The postmark of this postcard, a copy of which is held by the Internationale Gustav Mahler Gesellschaft.
[2] The *Münchner Neueste Nachrichten* newspaper.
[3] Oskar Merz, music critic of the *Nachrichten* who, along with other reviewers, had rejected *Guntram*—already sabotaged by part of the ensemble—after its only Munich performance on 16 November 1895.
[4] Heinrich Porges (1837–1900), writer on music and conductor of the Porgesscher Gesangverein which he founded.

Strauss to Mahler

> Munich
> 22 February 1897[1]

Dear Friend

Many thanks for sending me the Second [Symphony] (score and vocal score). The last movement, new to me, is a large structure indeed! How much I should like to hear the whole work, and still more to perform it! Behn's piano arrangement is a little masterpiece too.

I was so glad to have a small sign of life from you after so long; I had been thinking now and then that you had quite forgotten the first 'Mahlerian'!

> With best regards
> Ever yours
> Richard Strauss

---

[1] Postcard copied by Henry-Louis de La Grange.

Correspondence 1888–1911

Mahler to Strauss

Vienna
12 August 1897

Dear dear Friend

I come to you with a big request:

1. Have you an annotated vocal score or anything similar of *Rheingold*, from which I can see clearly how *Vogl*[1] plays Loge? (I feel sure you must have such notes in Munich.)
2. As far as I know, you have a *wooden trumpet* for the 'lustige Weise' in *Tristan* [Act III]. I should like to have one for Vienna.[2] To whom should I apply to have such an instrument made?

Please don't take it amiss that I don't write more. I am up to my eyes in work. How are you? Have you written anything new?

Cordial regards
Your old friend
Gustav Mahler

---

[1] Heinrich Vogl (1845–1903), singer at the Munich Court Opera. Strauss dedicated his songs, Op. 10, to him.

[2] Mahler had taken up his post as conductor of the Vienna Court Opera in May 1897 and was appointed Artistic Director in October 1897.

Strauss to Mahler

Knesebeckstrasse 30
Charlottenburg
22 April 1900[1]

Dear Friend

Have you a copy of the Austrian National Anthem with good orchestration in your archives? Of course!

Then I would ask you to have a copy of the score made at once (at the expense of the management here) and send it to me as soon as possible: we need it for 5 May. Our National Anthem (from a little printed book by H. Oertel) sounds wretched!

Many thanks in advance!

Could I take the opportunity to ask a question that you should answer by a short Yes or No and quite *sans gêne*, as I have had plenty of practice at receiving refusals from theatre directors. I am in the course of writing a one- or two-act burlesque ballet: *Kometentanz*,[2] an astral pantomime — naturally something departing wholly from the accustomed hopping-about — by Paul Scheerbart.[3]

Would you accept the ballet for the Vienna Opera, have the first performance and use some nice scenery? On the strength of my honest face?

If there is a chance of doing it anywhere else, I should prefer not to put on the first performance here in Berlin.

It will be ready to be performed about autumn 1901. — Please, a brief Yes or No: in the latter case without the usual phrases and excuses that I already know! —

Your songs, sung by Frau Herzog,[4] gave me and the audience much pleasure; but the establishment critics did not find them serious enough. Anything that does not contain a certain dose of boredom 'lacks style' at a concert.

A propos: has your Third Symphony already appeared in print? I should like to do 'What the flowers tell' from it next winter in Paris![5] As an introduction! Best regards for now. Please let me have the Anthem and a brief answer!

Ever yours
Richard Strauss

The directors of the Vienna Tantiemenanstalt[6] with Herr Weinberger[7] at their head are a fine crew! Don't let the publishers there get you down! Better discuss that by word of mouth! [Addendum to pp. 2 and 3 of the letter.]

Naturally, I only performed your songs so that you would be all the more sure to accept my ballet! That's the way I am! Well known for it! [Addendum to p. 4 of the letter.]

---

[1] The autograph of this letter is in the Gustav Mahler/Alfred Rosé Room, University of Western Ontario. Strauss had been Court Conductor at the Royal Opera in Berlin since the autumn of 1898, and lived in Charlottenburg.

[2] Strauss did not complete the composition.

[3] The German writer (1863–1915).

[4] Emilie Herzog (1859–1923) sang three orchestral songs by Mahler, conducted by Strauss, on 9 April 1900 in Berlin.

Correspondence 1888–1911

[5] The original title, later suppressed, of the second movement of Mahler's Third Symphony. Strauss did not, in fact, perform it in Paris.

[6] The Gesellschaft der Autoren, Komponisten und Musikverleger, a society of authors, composers and music publishers in Vienna, of which Mahler had been a member since 1897. Strauss, one of the founders of the Genossenschaft deutscher Tonsetzer, rejected the Vienna society because it included publishers (see pp. 132–3).

[7] Joseph Weinberger (1855–1928), head of the publishing house of that name, which brought out several works by Mahler.

Mahler to Strauss

[late April 1900]

in great haste!

Dear Friend

Your ballet is accepted *in advance*!—If I seem to attach a condition, it is only an elaboration of my unconditional agreement: I must have a look at the scenario mainly on account of the *cost* of the scenery. Could you let me see it, and also allow our set designers, wardrobe master, etc. to make a very rough estimate? In a few days you will have my answer, which you can then take as a binding acceptance.

What nice marginalia you add!? Good heavens! What experiences must you have had to risk the *manus lavat* allusion between us even in jest![1]— Please believe me that I am happy if I have an opportunity of showing your music the appreciation due to it.—That I have to educate the Viennese slowly to start with is only too natural after the decades of long, methodical stupefaction. That *I* am not vain, and am used to doing without the outward pleasures of authorship, you must have noticed.—I ask nothing of fate except a quiet little spot and a few weeks every year in which I can be entirely my own master and, if I am lucky, at least *one* good performance, so that I can once hear what I have done.—My warmest thanks for performing my trifles. I have read the scribblers, and come to my own conclusions. Always the same old song. You will not take it amiss if I ask you *not* to play a *single* movement from a symphony. It would be *too* misunderstood.

But I'll very gladly send you the Third Symphony! (Not so that you perform it, for I know that that would give rise to extreme difficulties—it lasts *two hours*.)

Regarding the National Anthem I shall do everything necessary straight

Correspondence 1888–1911

away. So, above all, *send the ballet at once*! I regard it as a *matter of honour* for the Vienna Court Opera to have the première. That you will be pleased with the production I can *guarantee*!

Sincerely yours
Mahler

---

[1] The expresssion *manus manum lavat* (lit. one hand washes the other), the equivalent of our 'I'll scratch your back and you scratch mine', refers to Strauss's sarcastic comment at the end of the previous letter that he only performed Mahler's songs to get Mahler to perform his ballet.

Mahler to Strauss

The Director
Imp. and Royal Court Opera
[summer or early autumn 1900][1]

Dear Friend

I have included your *Heldenleben* in the programme of one of this year's Phil. concerts[2] and am now asking whether you are willing and able to conduct it yourself. I think it is high time for you and our audience to become 'acquainted'.[3] Should you be willing, please let me have a time convenient to you — I would adhere to it if possible.

With best regards and in haste
Yours
Gustav Mahler

---

[1] On 14 October 1900 Strauss wrote to his parents: 'Mahler has invited me to conduct *Heldenleben* with the Philharmonic in Vienna on the 17th. Unfortunately, I had to refuse him performance and conducting, as I was under obligation to Herr Gutmann for 23 January.' (*RST Eltern*, p. 236.) The date given here indicates that at least one of Mahler's letters on this matter has been lost.

[2] From autumn 1898 to March 1901 Mahler conducted the Vienna Philharmonic Concerts. *Ein Heldenleben* symphonic poem, Op. 40 by Strauss, first performed 3 March 1899 in Frankfurt. It was not, in fact, performed in the 1900–1 Vienna Philharmonic Concert Season. Mahler only performed it in New York in 1911.

[3] In April 1895 Strauss had already conducted the Berlin Philharmonic in an invitation concert in Vienna. On 23 January 1901 Strauss appeared in Vienna at

Correspondence 1888–1911

the head of the Munich Kaim Orchestra to play his own works, including *Ein Heldenleben*. This concert was organized by the Albert Gutmann Agency.

Strauss to Mahler

Knesebeckstrasse 30
Charlottenburg
28 January 1901[1]

Dear Friend

Have received the Third![2] Many thanks! I must unfortunately save studying what seems, again, to be a very interesting creation for quieter times than the present, when I have to conduct daily (for Muck, who is ill, as well).[3]

That I, as an old connoisseur of scores, look forward tremendously to your symphony, I need not assure you! Once again, very many thanks!

I wrote today to Gustav Brecher:[4] he will approach you shortly. Receive him well! He is a very talented and cultivated man who, I am sure, will do you good service. Very best regards to you and your sister (from my wife also),

Yours very sincerely
R. Strauss

[1] The autograph of this letter is in the Ernest Rosé Collection.
[2] Mahler's Third Symphony, composed in 1895–6, only single movements being performed up to January 1901.
[3] Carl Muck (1859–1940), with Strauss a conductor at the Royal Opera, Berlin.
[4] Conductor and composer (1879–1940), engaged by the Vienna Opera 1901–2.

Mahler to Strauss

The Director
Imp. and Royal Court Theatre
[March/April 1901][1]

Dear Friend

I beg you only to send the *text*. Our *wardrobe master*, and the *set designer* and *technicians*, all of whom I engaged only a year ago and who are

50

outstanding modern artists, will give you great pleasure!—I am very sorry that you cannot have the première of your work in Vienna.—In general, I am not at all keen on 'first performances'. I do not care in the least how the journalists appraise an event at our institution. If I like a work, I accept it and perform it when I can.—But with your opera it is different. For it an exemplary model should be created; and *that* (I can say this to you without vaingloriousness) we, I am sure, are best able to put on the stage, with care and devotion and, most important of all, *without haste*. For that reason I must decline to become involved in a 'race' with another theatre. *Above all* in the interests of *your work*! Unless you yourself, after reflecting on what I have said, stand by your wish concerning the date. In that case I will do everything within my capability to give you the pleasure. (Between ourselves, in all things I believe the latter to be what matters—at most, allow me to share in it with you.)—

Fürstner should send the contracts at once. But please—for the sake of the negotiations, that are made much more difficult for me by the accounts office,—he should not be exorbitant in his usual way.—What matters is that we achieve *many* performances—therein lies every material advantage as well. So between us the matter is settled. I shall put on your work the moment circumstances guarantee a truly appropriate performance. If you nevertheless desire a date, I shall do all possible to fulfil your wish.—But if you can give us the *première*, I should of course put back everything else and guarantee the first performance for mid-November. In haste,

Yours sincerely
Mahler

I am still a little unsteady on my legs. I had haemorrhage in which I lost two-and-a-half litres of blood!

---

[1] The autograph of this undated letter is in the possession of Marius Flothuis, Amsterdam, but, as its history is unknown, it cannot be proved beyond doubt that it is addressed to Strauss. The contents and diction seem to indicate that it is one of the first letters relating to the Vienna performance of the opera *Feuersnot* by Strauss. The haemorrhage mentioned happened on 24 February 1901.

Correspondence 1888–1911

Mahler to Strauss

[June 1901]

Dear Friend

Feuersnot[1] is at the censor's. Once he passes it the agreements will be concluded. This is the official process required here.—On the date of the performance I can only decide after the season has started (end of August), when I can get an overall view. Would Bertram[2] in the main role be agreeable to you? In any case I must have *a vocal score* by the end of August to have a clear idea of the work and its performance.

The day after tomorrow I go on holiday. My address for the summer: Maiernigg am Wörthersee via Klagenfurt.[3]

With best regards
Yours ever
Gustav Mahler

---

[1] Strauss's one-act comic opera Op. 50, composed in 1900–1 and first performed in Dresden on 21 November 1901. It was a setting of the cautionary tale of Ernst von Wolzogen.
[2] Theodor Bertram (1869–1907), baritone.
[3] From 1901–7 Mahler spent his vacations at the villa built by him on the lakeside.

Strauss to Mahler

Allgemeiner Deutscher Musikverein[1]
[June 1901]

Confidential

Dear Friend

At next year's Festival [of the Allgemeiner Deutscher Musikverein] in Krefeld I should like to make your Third Symphony the main work![2] Naturally, you shall conduct it yourself! Has it already been performed anywhere?

Next winter I am conducting six concerts of new works here![3] Please let me know urgently whether your 'Titan' has appeared in print and whether it has already been performed in Berlin.

I should do your Third here too: but I am afraid I shall not be able to put the orchestra together for reasons of cost. I have eighty-five players (sixteen firsts, fourteen seconds, etc.) but only triple woodwinds and four horns: the reinforcements would cost about 300M and I am not sure that I can place this demand on the new enterprise. But then I might play your First!

Cordial regards
Yours
R. Strauss

---

[1] Strauss had just been elected President of the Allgemeiner Deutscher Musikverein (German Musical Society). The autograph of this undated letter is in the Maria Rosé Collection.

[2] Mahler's Third Symphony received its first performance on 9 June 1902 in Krefeld.

[3] In Berlin.

Mahler to Strauss

Maiernigg am Wörthersee
[Carinthia]
[June/July 1901]

Dear Friend

1. My First was performed in Berlin at my own concert—with the public largely excluded.[1]

2. My Third has *not yet been performed* at all—only two middle movements from it, including 'What the flowers tell me', which, torn from the whole at a Weingartner concert,[2] caused an immense misunderstanding of my intentions that truly horrified me.

Concerning *Feuersnot*, the *censor* seems, *horribile dictu*, to be making difficulties, since the work has not yet been passed, so that I am not in a position to send the contracts to Fürstner.

I fear you may have to accept changes. At any rate the 'lirum larum' will need changing,[3] not only the words themselves but probably more widely! Alas, there is still no placating these powers.

I shall of course pursue the matter and save what I can.

With very best wishes for the summer, to your wife as well,

Yours
Mahler

Correspondence 1888–1911

[1] A concert of Mahler's own compositions on 16 March 1896 in Berlin.

[2] Mahler is not quite accurate. In fact movements from the Third Symphony were performed at four concerts in 1896–7: on 9 November 1896 in Berlin Arthur Nikisch conducted the second movement; on 7 December 1896 in Hamburg Weingartner conducted the second movement, and, also under Weingartner, the second, third and sixth movements were performed in Berlin on 9 March 1897. Mahler himself conducted the second movement in Budapest on 31 March 1897.

[3] The great choral scene towards the end of *Feuersnot* contains the passage: 'Your god-forsaken prudery has stricken us with woe. There's no help in psalm-singing, nor in the men of cloth; the maid shall be the loser, lirum larum lei.'

Strauss to Mahler

Schweizerhof
Hôtel Suisse Interlaken
3 July 1901[1]

Dear Friend

I shall conduct six concerts[2] of new works in Berlin next winter and in the second, on 18 November, I shall perform your Third or—Fourth Symphony. Schillings[3] told me in Munich that you are writing a Fourth[4] that needs fewer performers than No. III.

Is that right? And if it is, would you let me have the Fourth for 18 November? I'll tell you why! The concerts are *on* the stage in the new Royal Opera House (Kroll) and I do not yet know whether I can position the boys' choir[5] at the proper height, get hold of the six bells, etc. I should certainly be able to procure the orchestra, and I have three weeks of rehearsals at my disposal.

The Third is already a definite prospect for the Festival in Krefeld, where they have a very large orchestra and a fine hall.

So please send me a line to say whether I might have your Fourth for 18 Nov. *this* year, assuming, of course, that it is really more convenient to perform than your Third.

I am here until 8 July and post will be forwarded after that. Please send a line here!

Very best regards
Yours
Rich. Strauss

Correspondence 1888–1911

[1] Autograph in the Bayerische Staatsbibliothek, Munich.
[2] With the Berlin Tonkünstlerorchester.
[3] Max von Schillings (1868–1933), composer and friend of Strauss's, active in the Allgemeiner Deutscher Musikverein.
[4] Mahler's Fourth Symphony, composed 1899–1901.
[5] For the fifth movement of the Third Symphony.

Mahler to Strauss

Maiernigg bei Klagenfurt
am Wörthersee
6 July 1901

Dear Friend

The Fourth is at the printer's! But I shall hardly have the parts ready by then, and there is another consideration. This is a new work—the first that may perhaps meet existing conditions in a rather more practical way and could, given an unprejudiced and sympathetic reception under favourable circumstances, bring me the only reward I desire from my creation: to be heard and understood.—I am reluctant to bring such a work before the Berlin audience, which does not know me and has been alienated from me in advance by a short-sighted press. I have promised Munich the first performance; and as there is even a 'scramble' for it there—*Kaim*[1] and Odeon[2] are vying for it—I have enough choices to agonise over as it is and beg you, my dear Strauss, not to let my Fourth enter your thoughts for the time being.

As far as the Third is concerned, I must insist that the performance matches my intentions exactly. The *six bells* are by no means the most important thing—they can well be dispensed with; perhaps there are four to be had—they would be enough. But the *acoustics* of the Kroll Hall are supposed to be *bad*!imo[3] Is it true? If so, dear friend, do nothing of mine there! The *orchestra* must be first-rate. The rehearsals must be very copious and—my work lasts two hours—there is room for nothing else in the programme. As in Krefeld, so in Berlin!

Please don't take it amiss if, to begin with, I meet your kind intentions with nothing but difficulties.—I know for certain that if it is within your power you will surmount these and I am at your disposal with utmost pleasure. And I have this further reason to plead for the Third, that I know at present of no one except you who could take on this monster. So, the Third! The Third!

Incidentally, if you have a *good* chorus at your disposal, there is also *Das klagende Lied*[4] which, of all my works, has so far made the most impression. It lasts 40 minutes. Perhaps one or other of the vocal pieces could be chosen with it. The chorus has a relatively small but very important and difficult part to play. If need be I could provide soloists.—Shall I send you the score, and where to?—

Now as regards your *Feuersnot*!

I have heard in a roundabout way that the censor is not releasing the work. Whether he is just making difficulties, or banning it, I have not yet found out. Unfortunately there is nothing to be done until September; then I shall go to see the censor myself; at present he is on vacation. I wonder whether the same thing will happen in Dresden. That would be dreadful! At any rate, I shall not give in.

With best wishes, and may your efforts be rewarded on high!

Yours most sincerely
Mahler

[1] A Munich orchestra founded by the Maecenas Franz Kaim.
[2] The concerts of the Musikalische Akademie took place in the Munich Odeon.
[3] About this time Mahler wrote to Bruno Walter from Maiernigg, '... how does the Kroll Hall sound? Strauss wants to do my Third there! Orchestra on the stage! Can it be done?' (*GML*, p. 253.)
[4] An early work by Mahler, completed 1880, first performed in revised form on 17 February 1901 in Vienna.

Strauss to Mahler

Grand Hotel und Kurhaus
Mürren
11 July [1901][1]

Dear Friend

What a pig-headed fellow you are! But it does no harm! It's just what is charming about you! It goes without saying that in Krefeld, where I hold absolute sway, your will is my command and your Third shall have a concert to itself!

For Berlin, however, where I work under difficult conditions and where it is impossible to ignore the financial side, I really would ask you to be more lenient. As the programme for 18 November I envisage:

Tasso[2] by Liszt—15–20 minutes
Love scene—finale—from *Feuersnot*—7 minutes
Mahler's Third two hours

Would you not agree even to this? If, as you say, there is as yet no understanding for your work in Berlin, the most important thing must be to get the public into the concert. I shall, of course, do nothing against your will, but I therefore ask you all the more earnestly to agree to the above programme *for Berlin*.

That I did not ask for the Fourth from vanity, to have the glory of a first performance, you will surely believe. I nevertheless flatter myself that I have more right to such a work than Herr Kaim or even the Munich Academy. And I should only want the Fourth if, *for the time being*, I am not quite able to perform the Third in accordance with your intentions, for they are what matter to me before all else. The Kroll acoustics are good. I do not yet know the chorus which is at my disposal, so that to begin with I should rather give it the small task in the Third than an entire choral work like *Das klagende Lied*. Please send me the score in any case; when I can place it properly, I shall be sure to do so.

When does the Fourth come out? If I find No. III too difficult, I shall take the Fourth in the second series of concerts, *after* Munich. The censor in Vienna is giving me enormous fun!

I dare not hope for a prohibition, since being banned by the censor would be the best advertisement the little opera could have, the more so because the Vienna performance would surely only be postponed, not cancelled. Or am I wrong?

So, please, when does No. IV appear?

And please send me the score of *Das klagende Lied* at Marquartstein in Upper Bavaria.

If the Vienna censor only objects to a few lines, we'll have another libretto printed and in place of the offending verses put asterisks with the footnote: for passage deleted by censor *see* vocal score.

That would sell in masses! Lucky publisher!

Sincere regards
Your old friend
Richard Strauss

Markus,³ the Prague conductor, asks me to commend him to you: I know him only as a good musician and a very decent chap, but unfortunately not as a conductor, so that I can only extend my recommendation as far as that. How do you like Brecher?⁴

Wasn't I right about Mikorey?⁵

[1] Transcript by Henry-Louis de La Grange.
[2] Symphonic poem by Franz Liszt.
[3] As yet unidentified.
[4] See p. 60.
[5] Franz Mikorey (1873–1947), a German conductor and composer from Munich. Strauss appears to have advised Mahler against engaging Mikorey.

Mahler to Strauss

[mid-July 1901]

Dear Friend
   Tasso 20
   Feuersnot 7
   Intervals 10
   Symphony two hours[1]

After the first movement *10 minutes* [interval] (absolutely necessary) — lasts more than *three hours*.

On top of that, the extraordinary demands the two new works place on the audience's attention and comprehension! Believe me, that would do *no* service to me and my work. I therefore suggest you drop my Third for Berlin this time, and perhaps do one of my innnumerable (and, if you like, still unpublished) vocal pieces, or again my Second, which only lasts one-and-a-half hours. This, however, should be in the Hall of the *Philharmonie*, as an organ is essential. — Otherwise you might do my Fourth. Perhaps in the second concert, as you proposed.

We need not decide anything yet, and in the autumn we shall act as the circumstances at the time demand. If you think my First (the so-called 'Titan') could be done, although it has already been performed — without an audience — in Berlin, I should have some confidence in the idea.

I shall have *Das klagende Lied* sent to you.

You are right about *Feuersnot*; it will be an enormous advertisement. But good heavens!—such works do not need advertising, which in my view, distracts attention from the work of art to superficial matters; and that is very regrettable. And finally, I have the delay, uncertainty with my arrangements, and a lot of annoyance and trouble.

So let us hope we may succeed in deflecting the austere censor from the path of virtue; for which may Eros and Dionysus give their blessing.— What have you against Bertram? He has *capital* high notes (up to F—even G), just as good as the low range, and is a fine, boisterous actor.— Otherwise, we have Demuth,[2] with a much better voice, to be sure, but— without the spark of genius!—For the female role I have *Schoder*[3] in mind and, for the second, Kurz,[4] who has a wonderful talent as a singer but insufficient acting ability.

With sincere regards
Yours
Mahler

The Fourth comes out in *October*.
There is a soprano solo in the last movement. Normal orchestra except for *four flutes* and an E-flat clarinet.
There are no trombones or tubas.

---

[1] The Third Symphony lasts on average 90 minutes. Perhaps Mahler exaggerated its length to persuade Strauss that it should be the only work in the programme.
[2] Leopold Demuth (1861–1910), baritone at the Vienna Court Opera.
[3] Marie Gutheil-Schoder (1874–1935), soprano at the Vienna Court Opera since 1900.
[4] Selma Kurz (1874–1933), coloratura soprano at the Vienna Court Opera since 1899.

Correspondence 1888–1911

Strauss to Mahler

Marquartstein
17 August 1901

Herr Hofoperndirector Gustav Mahler
Maiernigg am Wörthersee
nr Klagenfurt
Austria

Dear Friend

I have not yet received *Das klagende Lied*![1]

I have now fixed your Fourth for 15 December![2] How long does it last? It would probably be best to put it at the beginning of the programme?

Is Brecher still with you in Vienna? Are you satisfied with him?

The vocal score and choral parts for *Feuersnot* will reach you by 15 September at the latest. How goes it with the Lord High Censor?

Best regards
Yours
Rich. Strauss

[1] Postcard in the Maria Rosé Collection.
[2] The concert took place on 16 December 1901.

Mahler to Strauss

[Maiernigg]
[20? August 1901]

Dear Friend

I am going to Vienna on the 26th, and will find out something about the fate of our *Feuersnot*.—So far I only know that our highly moral Indendant,[1] who manages to be on equally good terms with the Graces, the nine muses and with our holy patron saints, wishes to inhibit the performance. All my representations and appeals to 'common sense' seem to have been in vain.—Vederemo!

Brecher is a capital and likable fellow, but for us he is too short of experience and practical skill. I shall try to get him leave of absence to spend one or two seasons at a municipal theatre somewhere. Regarding my Fourth there are a number of doubts that come to my mind: the work is conceived in a rather *concertante* manner for wind and strings, and needs especially sensitive players.—From what I read, you have a new orchestra, the quality of which leaves much to be desired! Will they be equal to a work of this kind, that is by no means alfresco but full of fine shading.

It lasts about 45 minutes, starts *pp*—finishes *pp*—and hardly has a real *ff* anywhere, so that it should probably be placed in the middle of the concert.

I shall have *Das klagende Lied* sent to you as soon as I reach Vienna.

Sincerest regards in the meantime

Yours
Mahler

[1] August Freiherr Plappart von Leenheer, General Intendant of the Hoftheater, 1898–1906.

Mahler to Strauss

The Director
Imp. and Royal Court Opera
[late November/early December 1901][1]

Dear Friend

Though I know you to be hard at work, I must disturb you for a moment to say that the material for my symphony can only be sent off on Wednesday 4th (by express), and so will only be in Berlin on the 5th [December]. Whether this will be a serious interruption for you I cannot judge, since I do not know how your rehearsals are arranged. If I attend the last three rehearsals, will that be enough? When should I arrive?

On your *Feuersnot*, which has finally been passed here, and which I want to perform at the beginning of January,[2] I shall have to confer with you at length.

Only this for today, in haste,

Yours
Mahler

[1] Autograph in the Gemeentemuseum, The Hague.
[2] The performance did not, in fact, take place until 29 January.

Correspondence 1888–1911

Mahler to Strauss

The Director
Imp. and Royal Court Opera
[between 4 and 8 December 1901][1]

Dear Friend

I arrive in Berlin on Tuesday morning, and am staying at the *Pallasthotel*. Could we have a rendezvous the same day? I don't mind when or where!—By an oversight two sets of parts have been sent to you. Please use the one sent to you from *Vienna* (Eberle & Co).[2] You will find the *'little bells'* instrument in the parcel sent by Weingartner;[3] I arranged for this as I think you are unlikely to have such an instrument—used only for ballets—in your orchestra.

How does Destinn view the solo part?[4] I have not yet had any answer from her. I should like to rehearse a little with her in Berlin! When? Where? Would it not be a good idea for me to take one rehearsal myself in your presence, for which I should need a whole morning? Unfortunately the conductor's notes are often inadequate, as I found in Munich! We'll talk about everything on Wednesday![5]

Sincerely
Mahler

---

[1] Mahler arrived in Berlin on Tuesday 10 December.

[2] The Vienna printer of Mahler's Fourth Symphony, published by Ludwig Doblinger, Vienna.

[3] The sleigh bells used in various places in the Fourth Symphony, notably at the start of the first movement. Weingartner had gone on a tour of South German cities with the Fourth Symphony.

[4] Emmy Destinn (1878–1930), soprano, appears to have been intended for the solo which, however, was finally sung by Thila Plaichinger (1868–1939).

[5] On Wednesday 11 December 1901 Mahler wrote from Berlin to his sister Justine: 'Rehearsed today! Everything is going capitally and I am conducting the *performance* myself, as I agreed with Strauss today'. (*Gustav Mahler, Unbekannte Briefe* edited by Herta Blaukopf, Paul Zsolnay Verlag, Vienna and Hamburg, 1983, p. 116.)

Correspondence 1888–1911

Mahler to Strauss

The Director
Imp. and Royal Court Opera
[early January 1902]

Dear Friend

Programme etc. are being sent off with this letter. All is arranged so that you need only sit down and conduct. Perhaps we shall speak further about it when you are here; we both agree that only the performance matters. You can take my word that I have no conductor's vanity.

At any rate you must conduct one performance or another here. Whether the première or a later one depends on how our personnel follow your baton.

I have prepared everything with devotion and ignored none of your hints.—As far as details are concerned, all is ready. The first (solely musical) general rehearsal [of *Feuersnot*] is tomorrow—a so-called *Sitzprobe* concerned only with musical adjustments. Looking forward with great pleasure to seeing you soon,

Yours very sincerely
Mahler

Strauss to Mahler

Berlin
[5 January 1902][1]

Dear Friend

How goes *Feuersnot*?

Could the première be on the 29th?

I could then arrive early on the 27th for the last two rehearsals. You know that I have concerts on the 30th and 31st in Vienna,[2] and that I would be immensely grateful to you if you could make everything very much easier for me by having the first performance on the 29th.

For the preliminary study I should mention that up to now it has always proved necessary in the ensemble (vocal score Nos. 172–7) to double Walpurg in the high range with some powerful chorus sopranos and similarly with the singers of Margret and Elsbeth. Likewise, Walpurg should be backed by a number of chorus sopranos from Nos. 209–11!!

Fig. 1   Mahler, caricature and silhouette by Hans Schliessmann.

Correspondence 1888–1911

What do you say of the St Vitus's dance which your Fourth incited in the Berlin critics? I must say it has far exceeded my worst expectations.

Heartfelt congratulations, from my wife too, on your engagement:[3] this will put you in the very best spirits for the *Feuersnot* rehearsals, so that I can congratulate myself as well.

Best regards to your fiancée
Your ever devoted
Richard Strauss

---

[1] Strauss actually wrote, incorrectly, 5 January 1901. The autograph is in the Haus-, Hof- und Staatsarchiv, Vienna, Hof-Operntheater, No. 48/1902.

[2] On 30 January 1902 Ernst von Possart recited the melodrama 'Enoch Arden', Op. 38, by Strauss; on 31 January Pauline Strauss-de Ahna sang songs by Strauss. Both were accompanied by the composer at the piano.

[3] Mahler had become engaged to Alma Maria Schindler in December 1901.

Mahler to Strauss

The Director
Imp. and Royal Court Opera
[early or mid-January 1902]

Dear Friend

Everything has been arranged in accordance with your wishes. Première on the *29th*, dress rehearsal on the 28th. But would it not be better to let us conduct?[1] For I am afraid that if you take this difficult work over with one rehearsal, our players might be disconcerted. Could you not, as agreed, come at least a week earlier? In haste,

Yours sincerely,
Mahler

---

[1] Mahler conducted the première and the subsequent performances.

Correspondence 1888–1911

Strauss to Mahler

Charlottenburg
4 February 1902[1]
8 p.m.!

My dear Friend

I do not know a finer hour than this, when you are conducting the second performance of *Feuersnot*, to send you once more my most heartfelt thanks for the incomparably beautiful rendition you gave of my work last week, and will, I hope, often give again.

I still revel in the recollection of the magical sound of the orchestra, the magnificent décor created by the genius of Brioschi and Löffler [*sic*],[2] the glorious poetry of sound with which the soloists and chorus delighted my ear.

As it was not possible for me to thank all those involved personally on the evening of the 29th, could I ask you to be so kind as to convey on a suitable occasion, to all who have taken such extraordinary pains with my work, apart from all the soloists, chorus and orchestra, Herr Brioschi and Herr Löffler already mentioned, especially the stage-manager, Herr Stoll,[3] and the conductor of the chorus, Herr Luze,[4] not to forget the all-important producer of the 'Feuersnot'[5]—(I mean, of course, the lighting manager)—my warmest thanks, resounding in all the registers of admiration.

If *Feuersnot* is still alive then, I shall come to hear the work again when passing through Vienna on 21 March, if you would be kind enough to hold the performance that day.

With cordial regards and in sincerest gratitude,

Your ever devoted
Richard Strauss

---

[1] Autograph in the Haus-, Hof- und Staatsarchiv, Vienna, Hof-Operntheater, No. 48/1902.

[2] Anton Brioschi (1855–1920) designed the set for *Feuersnot*, Heinrich Lefler (1863–1919) the costumes. Lefler was manager of scenery at the Court Opera from 1900–3. Designers' names were not given on the Vienna programmes at this time, so Strauss may not have seen Lefler written down.

[3] August Stoll (1853?–1918), stage-manager at the Court Opera 1885–1918. In most of the works he conducted Mahler involved himself in the stage-management.

[4] Karl Luze conductor of the chorus.
[5] *Feuersnot* (lit. 'fire famine') takes its name from a spell by which all flames are extinguished and the stage is plunged in darkness.

Mahler to Strauss

The Director
Imp. and Royal Court Opera
18 February [1902]

Dear Friend

I am so disgusted by the attitude of the Viennese press,[1] and most of all by the public's total acquiescence to them, that I cannot get over it. How I should love to throw it all down at their feet!—The proceeds of the performances are as follows:

I   3,100 fl
II 1,600 fl
III 1,300 fl

IV—Carnival Monday—*one of the best days of the year—900!* (was cancelled at the last moment!)

Alas, alas, I must take the work off for the present. But I shall not give in!—On 4 April we have a *new ballet*—I shall put on *Feuersnot* with it, they will all have to be there again and—we shall see! Perhaps we shall have a less prejudiced gathering.

If this does not come off, in the autumn I shall dig out a one-acter (though Demuth must not be involved in it), and so I shall try and try again. It drives one to despair to be at the mercy of this Areopagus of narrow-minded meanness without any right of appeal.—At the première I still had some hopes.—This, alas, dear friend, is all I can tell you for now of the fate of your child (and my own child of sorrow)—I hope I shall have happier news in April. In haste,

Yours very sincerely
Mahler

[1] 'The critics have unanimously rejected the work, it was salvo after salvo from right to left, conservatives and radicals.' (Max Graf in *Die Musik*, 1 March 1902, p. 1023.)

Correspondence 1888–1911

Mahler to Strauss

The Director
Imp. and Royal Court Opera
21 February [1902]

Dear Friend

How wrong you are! *1*. Not three performances—there were four,[1] with very eloquent attendance figures. *2*. To continue to perform an opera when the *whole* audience stays away does not depend on my *goodwill*, which I hope you will not doubt. The management would immediately *veto* it.— Our audience being what it is—I know it very exactly—there is certainly *nothing* to be done at present. At the fifth performance the theatre would be empty! I know this *from experience*! No matter what I put on with it!

However, as you have expressed your wish so decidedly, I shall put the work on once more with *Cavalleria* or *Hansel*. (*Bajazzo* [Pagliacci] isn't possible, as Demuth cannot sing two parts.) But you will see—this *really would* damage the work!—I am also afraid that I shall not get permission from the management (or still *higher up*).[2]—I am myself perhaps in no less consternation than you, but to fight against impossible odds is, after all— impossible!

Most faithfully yours
Mahler

[1] There were actually only three: Mahler is probably including the cancelled one of 10 February.
[2] The Supreme Court Steward's Office, which had jurisdiction over the Vienna Opera.

Mahler to Strauss

The Director
Imp. and Royal Court Opera
[28 February 1902]

Dear Friend

Today a small one-act opera[1] of which I expect a 'success' (it is really charming and original) is going on stage. If it does well, I shall put *Feuersnot* on with it on 19 March, and ask you to conduct it yourself. A rehearsal will be fixed at your convenience. Please let me know in the course of *this week* whether I can count on you, as I am absent for the second half of March[2] and must make my arrangements for that day now.

If this comes off, we shall have a pair that would be particularly agreeable to me in that Pegasus would not be yoked to a mere carthorse.

In great haste,

Yours very sincerely
Mahler

---

[1] *Der dot mon*, a carnival play by Hans Sachs, with music by Joseph Forster, which had its Viennese première on 28 February 1902.

[2] Mahler went on a concert tour to St Petersburg with his young wife.

Mahler to Strauss

The Director
Imp. and Royal Court Opera
[early March 1902]

Dear Friend

The new work won't do either! It had quite a good reception, but won't gallop away.—I shall therefore put on *Feuersnot* on 14 March with a very popular ballet that has not been performed for a *long* time.[1]

This is not possible, unfortunately, on the 21st! But I shall put *Feuersnot* on with a new work[2] in April, to which I should like to invite you. You will hear more at the end of March.

Hoping to see you again soon,

Yours
Mahler

---

[1] *Rund um Wien* by Josef Bayer.

[2] The ballet *Die Perle von Iberien* by Josef Hellmesberger jun., which had its première on 7 April and was performed with *Feuersnot* for the first time on 19 April 1902. On 20 April Strauss wrote to his parents 'Today I received the very gratifying news from Mahler that the fifth performance of *Feuersnot* with a popular new ballet turned out very well and that he now hopes to keep the work on.' (*RST Eltern*, p. 257.) Mahler's letter to Strauss has not been preserved.

Correspondence 1888–1911

Mahler to Strauss

The Director
Imp. and Royal Court Opera
[early May 1902]

Dear Friend

I have not answered your last, kind letter as I have been waiting for an answer from Müller-Reuter[1] to a letter in which I set out a programme of rehearsals, which agrees with yours apart from a few details.

I recapitulate:

In Cologne:
1) 3 June rehearsals morning and afternoon with the *full* orchestra
2) 4 June—*ditto* (one rehearsal in the morning, one in the afternoon) then in *Krefeld*
3) *Friday* morning, from 9, so I can work with fresh performers for *three* hours.
4) Sunday, *all morning* (four hours) and finally
5) Monday, final rehearsal of two hours. *On this* I *must* insist.

When you talk about your experience in Berlin with the *Fourth*, you forget that this work lasts three-quarters of an hour and is *easy*, whereas my Third lasts *two* hours and is *difficult* and unusual.—Furthermore, this is the *first performance* and everything in my immediate future depends on it! I assure you, I don't mind waiting! But it is *unbearable* to me to send my work into the world without sufficient preparation, and to add a confused and deficient performance to the difficulties and obstacles arising from my astringent intentions, which are hard to understand as it is. Believe me, for this work I *must* have a faultless performance. Otherwise you will do me grave harm, instead of helping me and smoothing my path, as you undoubtedly intend. Therefore: you *must* secure me these rehearsals, and I cannot do without any of them. Otherwise, however sorry I should be, I could not collaborate. Concerning the question of costs, I admit that this time your kind help is very welcome. Nevertheless, I am always ready to make sacrifices if they must be asked of me, and I know you will not demand more than is absolutely necessary. But I say this again for guidance, should you encounter difficulties in your Sunday session. About the *quality* of the orchestra I am, I must admit, no less concerned after your last letter! To increase the thirty-strong Krefeld orchestra to a hundred? Where from? And how? A motley collection that is not up to standard could not cope with

Correspondence 1888–1911

my work; that I know! Just have a look at the score! At any rate, the first trombone must be outstanding, with a colossal tone and mighty breath! Would not your first trombonist in Berlin, whom I have heard highly praised, be best for this?

Now it is all in your hands, dear Friend, and as soon as you have made any decision on my fate on Sunday, please put my mind at rest!

I was immensely glad about *Feuersnot*. I shall not give up now. The next performance (the ninth) is on Friday the 23rd of the month![2] — In the autumn *you* must conduct it here.

With sincere regards
Yours
Mahler

The alto solo[3] is going off to Lessmann[4] tomorrow. I also sent it to Müller-Reuter a few weeks ago to be forwarded to the singer!

---

[1] Theodor Müller-Reuter (1858–1919), conductor of the Concert Society in Krefeld from 1893–1918.

[2] *Feuersnot* was performed only once in May, on the 7th.

[3] From the fourth movement of Mahler's Third Symphony, which was first performed on 9 June 1902 at the Festival in Krefeld.

[4] Otto Lessmann (1844–1918), music critic and composer, an official in the Allgemeiner Deutscher Musikverein.

Strauss to Mahler

Marquartstein
Upper Bavaria[1]
21 July [1902][2]

Herr Gustav Mahler from Vienna
Maiernigg (Wörther See)
Carinthia

Dear Friend

As you need a horn player, — my father,[3] whom I am just visiting, recommends one: *Max Müller, first horn at the Spa Orchestra* at *Bad Reichenhall*.

I have written to Herr Müller, saying he should apply direct to you. Perhaps you could have the young man come to Vienna and blow for you!

Correspondence 1888–1911

How are you otherwise? Contented and industrious? How long does *Das klagende Lied* last? Is it very difficult for the chorus? I should like to do it this winter in Berlin! How is your dear wife?

Best regards to you both
Your old friend
R. Strauss

---

[1] The de Ahna family had a country residence here, in Upper Bavaria where Strauss spent his vacations.
[2] Autograph (postcard) in the Haus-, Hof- und Staatsarchiv, Vienna, Hof-Operntheater, No. 515/1902.
[3] Franz Joseph Strauss (1822–1905), previously first French horn in the Munich Court Orchestra.

Mahler to Strauss

The Director
Imp. and Royal Court Opera
[late January/early February 1903][1]

Dear Friend

My contract with my present publisher is such a muddle (I, at least, cannot find my way in it) that I do not know whether I am entitled to join the *Genossenschaft* deutscher Tonsetzer.[2] For I have put myself under obligation to join the *Society of Authors here*.[3] (At the time, in order to be published I would not have minded joining a Society for the Preservation of Purgatory.) Shall I send you my contract? And could you or your experts glean the necessary from it? — If it is all right, I should be most glad to be a member of your society and, of course, to sit on the committee. — Would it not be best for us to discuss it all when *you are here*, and for you to keep open my right to membership until then? — Apart from that, my wife asks you both to lunch with us (followed by a nap in a quiet room) and to be with us after the concert. *Quite alone* and undisturbed.

Sincerely yours
Mahler

---

[1] The following postcard from Strauss is no doubt to be seen as a direct answer to the invitation extended here.

Correspondence 1888–1911

[2] The Guild of German Composers, in the founding of which Strauss played a major part, was incorporated in 1903.
[3] The Gesellschaft der Autoren, Komponisten und Musikverleger in Vienna. Mahler was admitted on 11 November 1897 and resigned on 31 December 1903 at Strauss's instigation, in order to join the Genossenschaft deutscher Tonsetzer (see pp. 132–3).

Strauss to Mahler

5 February 1903[1]

[...] I only arrive in Vienna at 1.10 on 4 March. If half-past two suits you for your midday meal, I should come with great pleasure. Perhaps, however, as I have an informal rehearsal in the afternoon, it would be better in the evening, after the concert![2] [...] Is *Feuersnot* still alive? [...]

[1] Quoted in the Autographen-Auktionskatalog No. 606 (1975), by J. A. Stargardt, Marburg. According to the catalogue, this is a postcard addressed to Alma Mahler.
[2] On 4 March 1903 Strauss conducted a concert by the Berlin Tonkünstlerorchester.

Strauss to Mahler

Berlin
27 November 1904[1]

Dear Friend

Just back from my travels, I am writing to thank you and the committee of the Society[2] for your kind telegram, and to thank you especially for the wonderful performance you gave of the work.[3] The more thankless such a task is in kindling transient Viennese enthusiasm, the less shall I forget what you have done. Best regards to you and your dear wife,

Yours sincerely
Dr Richard Strauss

[1] Transcript by Alma Mahler.

Correspondence 1888–1911

[2] The *Vereinigung schaffender Tonkünstler in Wien*, founded in 1904 with Mahler as its Honorary President.

[3] *Symphonia domestica*, Op. 53 by Strauss, first performed on 21 March 1904 under Strauss in New York. Its first performance in Vienna was at the first orchestral concert of the *Vereinigung schaffender Tonkünstler* on 23 November 1904 under Mahler.

Strauss to Mahler

15 February 1905[1]

Dear Friend

I have just learned through Frau Hermann Wolff[2] that on Sunday we shall have the pleasure of welcoming you here personally[3] for the first performance of your Fifth.

That's capital!

As you are (alas!) not conducting yourself,[4] I am sure you will give me the pleasure, on

Monday 20th at 1.30 p.m.

to come with your wife and have a cosy meal with us, to which we both look forward. With best regards from us both,

Your ever devoted
Richard Strauss

Please send a few consenting words to Joachimsthalerstrasse 17, Berlin W15.

---

[1] Postcard transcribed by Alma Mahler.
[2] Louise (Aloysia) Wolff (1855–1935), who managed the Hermann Wolff Concert Bureau after her husband's death.
[3] Mahler did not, in fact, go to Berlin on this occasion.
[4] Arthur Nikisch (1855–1922) conducted Mahler's Fifth Symphony at the Philharmonic Concert on 20 February 1905.

Correspondence 1888–1911

Strauss to Mahler

Berlin
5 March 1905[1]

Dear Friend

Many thanks for your delightful letter[2] and all your kind help: please send your exact programme[3] to our Secretary and Herr Rösch[4] as soon as possible, with names of singers, and enclose the texts for the programme. And the voice-types of the soloists not known to me; we should, of course, be very glad if we could use some or all of them for the other programme. For the *Requiem* by Josef Reiter[5] and the *Te Deum* by Bruckner we need the usual oratorio quartet; for the one-hour choral work by Otto Naumann[6] a dramatic singer with an outstanding voice (mezzo-soprano), and for the rest of the programme a very good baritone. The Festival conductor is Ferdinand Löwe,[7] who will come to an understanding with you directly about all the instrumentalists whom, thanks to your kindness, he may draw from the Court Orchestra.[8]

Feuersnot I shall gladly conduct myself, on the 27th.

The letter to your Intendant will likewise go off very soon.

Your Fifth Symphony again gave me great pleasure in the full rehearsal, a pleasure only slightly dimmed by the little Adagietto. But as this was what pleased the audience most, you are getting what you deserve.

The first two movements, especially, are quite magnificent; the Scherzo has a quality of genius but seemed rather too long; how far the somewhat inadequate performance was responsible, I was unable to judge. At the final rehearsal your work had a great and unclouded success. The concert audience, by contrast, showed themselves somewhat more indolent intellectually, which is nothing new to you or me. Nikisch set to work with much zeal and, as far as German music suits him at all, in my opinion acquitted himself very well.

So please let me know soon about the kind and ability of the soloists for your songs etc. Best regards to you and your wife,

Your ever devoted
Richard Strauss

My wife sends her greetings.

---

[1] Transcript by Alma Mahler.
[2] As yet, undiscovered.

Correspondence 1888–1911

³ For the Festival in Graz, 31 May to 4 June 1905.
⁴ Friedrich Rösch (1862–1925), musician and lawyer, active in the Allgemeiner Deutscher Musikverein and the Genossenschaft deutscher Tonsetzer.
⁵ Josef Reiter (1862–1939), an Austrian composer.
⁶ *Der Tod und die Mutter* for soloists, 12-part choir and large orchestra by Otto Naumann (1871–1932), a German composer.
⁷ Ferdinand Löwe (1865–1925), conductor.
⁸ i.e. the Court Opera Orchestra.

Mahler to Strauss

The Director
Imp. and Royal Court Opera
[late April 1905]¹

Dear Friend

I am rehearsing *Feuersnot* with a *new* cast.²
Diemuth—Frl. Förstel³
Kunrad—Herr Weidemann⁴
Both have splendid voices and are original, spirited players.—I hope the performance will give you pleasure. As I have now to make my arrangements (everything must be ready *before* I leave for Strasbourg),⁵ please tell me definitively whether I should fix it for 5 [deleted: May] *June* or 27 May, as was decided originally, and *when* you can hold the final rehearsal.—As I have heard nothing for weeks, I do not know where I am. The singers for my songs are *Weidemann, Moser*⁶ (baritones) and *Sembach*,⁷ tenor.

Sincerely, in great haste
Mahler

¹ On 28 April Strauss wrote to Max von Schillings, 'As soloists Mahler has the baritones Weidemann and Moser, and the tenor Sembach...'
² The Vienna Court Opera offered the participants in the Graz Festival three performances on their return, including *Feuersnot*.
³ Gertrude Förstel (1880–1950).
⁴ Friedrich Weidemann (1871–1919).
⁵ Venue of the Alsatian Musical Festival 20–2 May, 1905, where Strauss and Mahler conducted their own works (see pp. 134 f.).
⁶ Anton Moser (1872–1909).
⁷ Johannes Sembach (1881–1944).

Correspondence 1888-1911

Strauss to Mahler

Berlin W. 15
5 May 1905[1]

Dear Friend

I have to give you two pieces of bad news at once; as I have to conduct the *Festwiese*[2] at the Crown Prince's Wedding on 5 June (as if Wagner had composed it only for such occasions!), I must leave Graz on 4 June.

For this reason I cannot conduct, firstly, *Feuersnot* in Vienna on the 5th, and ask if *you* could do it for me, and secondly, the *Heldenleben* on the 4th in Graz, which has therefore been moved to 2 June and must be replaced on the 4th by Liszt's *Ideale* as the opening number of the last concert (yours). This brings me to the main point of this letter: the gentlemen at Graz have told me often that you would like a concert of your own in Graz for your songs, which last one-and-a-quarter hours. Up to now I have taken this as a piece of somewhat exaggerated festival zeal on the part of the Graz Opera composers *vis-à-vis* the Director of the Vienna Court Opera. I have taken all the less notice of it as you yourself have never expressed such a wish to me, and even once asked me not to perform your Fifth Symphony at Graz so that you could support the Festival without being suspected of ulterior motives by your superiors. This would be still more the case if I were now to allocate you a whole concert for a series of songs lasting one-and-a-quarter hours. As I was accused two years ago by a number of deservedly unperformed fellow artists of giving preferential treatment to compositions by Mahler, I am anxious to avoid an appearance of partiality, the more so because I have, as President, obligations towards the entire membership; and because—which is the main thing—the special position you desire does not on this occasion seem to me artistically necessary. What objections do you now have to a programme like this:

1. *Ideale* by Liszt (20 minutes), only to warm up the audience as an introduction, then
2. One-and-a-quarter hours Mahler songs
3. Imperial March [Wagner] as conclusion.

A finer programme, or one more favourable to you, I cannot imagine! Your songs are the principal attraction of the programme, and the two old gentlemen provide the framework!

I hope you are in agreement. You know I am glad to oblige you at all times, but on this occasion I really could not meet your wish for a matinée of your own, for on 4 June there is the second Chamber Music morning, on 3 June the morning is completely filled by the General Assembly. An extension of the Festival by a day is absolutely impossible.

We can discuss details when we meet in Strasbourg. Is it still the arrangement that we shall have twenty-four soloists from the Vienna Court Orchestra as support for the *whole* Graz Festival, especially for *Heldenleben* on 2 June?

I have personally sent invitations to your singers Gutheil,[3] Kittel,[4] Weidemann and Preuss.[5]

Please send your song texts by return to Graz for censorship and to us for printing in the programme, that has to be produced very urgently.

Best regards
Yours sincerely
Dr Richard Strauss

[1] Transcript by Alma Mahler.
[2] Act III of *Die Meistersinger*.
[3] See p. 59.
[4] Hermine Kittel (1876–1948), alto.
[5] Arthur Preuss (1878–1944), tenor.

Mahler to Strauss

The Director
Imp. and Royal Court Opera
[between 6 and 9 May 1905]

My programme would last about half an hour.

Dear Friend

I do not desire a 'special position'! That would be a great misunderstanding on your part. Only a *small hall* for my songs that would be performed in the manner of *chamber music.*—And just because I should not wish to take away an *evening*, I suggest a matinée. And in the interests of the *whole* it does not seem dignified to put on a few songs as the *conclusion* of a *Festival*.

So please think it over again! 'Preferential treatment' for Mahler? Should an artistic association really have *democratic* principles? Or should the gentlemen regard your espousal of my cause as camaraderie? Both assumptions are repugnant to me! Moreover, you yourself know best that I am not forcing myself upon you, and that I really am not vain.—Here, for artistic reasons (despite all the pressure of 'commercial' considerations), I have put on these songs only in the *small* hall, and they were only appropriate there.[1] To perform them in a large hall[2] to round off a Festival is *decidedly lacking in taste* and really would expose us to those reproaches! For the rest (as I in no way wish to cause embarrassment and, believe me, would like *very much* to withdraw completely) I bow to your decision, but ask you to give serious consideration to my arguments.—Your request for confidentiality I must surely not understand as meaning that I may not make any use of what you have told me about programme changes? I have to make the necessary provisions at once.—And here is the second *difficulty*. If *I conduct Feuersnot* here on the 5th instead of you, I cannot possibly be in Graz on the 4th! You know how difficult your work is, if one does not want to confuse the notes (in what the critics call 'bold strokes'!). The main parts have new performers! I shall do everything to have the work ready in good time. But whether I can hold the final rehearsal so early that I can stay in Graz on 2, 3 and 4 May [Mahler meant June] I do not know at present.—If I have the matinée on 4 May I can hold the final rehearsal here with Weidemann (who sings the *Lieder* there) the following morning and with only a minor further change to the programme (*Elisabeth*[3] on the 5th) I could conduct *Feuersnot* on the 6th! So please let me know now what you think and can do.—For my part I agree to everything.

I am counting on you to conduct the new production of *Feuersnot* here personally as this would be very helpful in propagating the work and getting it accepted by the theatre-going public.

With sincere regards and looking forward to seeing you again,

Yours
Mahler

NB I should say that I should have preferred to be entirely free in Graz in order to devote myself more fully to my Vienna tasks and also, as you mention, in order not to appear *self-seeking*.—But as Schillings felt he had to insist on something of mine being performed in Graz, I suggested the songs, as they are less trouble to prepare, being a more modest gift.

But as they *are* being performed, it must be done in appropriate style. So—only in the small hall!

That I should cut a better figure at a large festival concert is self-evident. So it cannot be ostentation on my part to prefer a matinée in the small hall.—

Correspondence 1888–1911

Your wishes concerning *twenty-four* Philharmonic players will meet no difficulties from me.—However, the committee (I believe for financial reasons) seems to want to engage a smaller number.

[1] On 29 January 1905 the *Vereinigung schaffender Tonkünstler in Wien* had organized a Mahler evening in the small Music Society Hall, at which the *Kindertotenlieder* and four other Rückert songs were given their first performance.

[2] In the Industry Hall in Graz.

[3] Franz Liszt's oratorio *Die Legende von der heiligen Elisabeth*, which Mahler never, in fact, conducted. The performance was conducted by Franz Schalk on the 7th, not the 5th, of June.

Mahler to Strauss

The Director
Imp. and Royal Court Opera
[about 10 May 1905]

Dear Friend

As *Löwe* will have written to you by now, a way out has been found. As the first concert takes place on 1 June in the *Stephanie* Hall (the room suited to my pieces), things have been rearranged to provide a place for me. I hope all is now in order.—To me this is particularly agreeable for *Weidemann*'s sake, as he can have a good rest after 1 May [Mahler means June], and I have time for two proper orchestral rehearsals of *Feuersnot*. Weidemann is a splendid fellow and exactly the right artist to do justice to your work, and so, I hope, to keep it in our repertoire.—

Once I have your agreement I shall send the texts to Lessmann.

Best regards, in haste
Yours very sincerely
Mahler

I have just received your telegram! My songs last one-and-a-half hours and with two other numbers fill the first concert. *Weidemann*, *Moser* and *Sembach* are the singers.[1]

[1] On 1 June 1905 thirteen songs by Mahler were performed in Graz: six songs from *Des Knaben Wunderhorn*, the *Kindertotenlieder* and two other Rückert songs. The singers were Friedrich Weidemann, Anton Moser, Fritz Schrödter (1855–1924), tenor, and Erik Schmedes (1868–1931), tenor. Johannes Sembach did not take part.

Strauss to Mahler

Marquartstein
Upper Bavaria
18 August 1905[1]

Dear Friend

Have you really the intention announced in the enclosed notice from *Der Tag*?[2] If so, I should at least like to let you know that by 1 September the Fürstner publishing firm will have finished preparing the vocal scores[3] and proofs, from which the study of the main parts can be begun. Schuch[4] is starting on 1 September and expects to bring the work out about the end of November. The orchestral material ought, by human calculation, to be ready by 1 November.

If you therefore agree a contract by return with Fürstner (who will not otherwise supply you with parts) you can, if you think fit, start studying the main parts at the beginning of September; it is likely to take two to three weeks. For Herodes, Herodias and Jochanaan the probable choices are Schmedes, Mildenburg[5] and Weidemann. Narraboth—Slezak.[6] Now, what of Salome? For Dresden I have decided after all on Frau Wittich[7] (for style and power of voice). Do you not think that for Vienna Frl. Kurz[8] would be suitable? I have heard from many quarters that she is your best voice. She is certainly pretty. Has she acting talent?

I have had enthusiastic reports of your songs in Graz from many friends (Rösch).[9] Your *Feuersnot* is said to have been wonderful too. Many thanks retrospectively.

Schmedes sang a very respectable Tristan in Cologne. But I was very disappointed with Mildenburg's Isolde (apart from Act I, where she had great moments). Voice, intonation and diction left almost everything to be desired in Acts II and III. Kittel was vocally excellent, and Meyer[10] very sound.

How are you otherwise? Is the Seventh finished already?[11]

I stay here until 1 October and am hoping to have good news from you soon.

With sincerest regards to you and your wife, from mine too. (To whom does she owe the kind gift of soap—many thanks!)

Yours ever
Dr Richard Strauss

Please take care in ordering the scenery that it is as low as possible and the acoustics favourable. Massive sets are not needed, Jochanaan's cistern that juts above ground should be so arranged that the singer can sing and see the conductor through a hole concealed with gauze and invisible to the audience.

[1] Transcript by Alma Mahler.
[2] Announcing the intention to perform *Salome* at the Vienna Opera.
[3] For *Salome*, Strauss's opera Op. 54, based on the play by Oscar Wilde.
[4] Conductor of the Dresden Opera (see p. 26).
[5] Anna von Mildenburg (1872–1947), dramatic soprano, at the Vienna Opera since 1898.
[6] Leo Slezak (1873–1946), tenor.
[7] Marie Wittich (1868–1931), dramatic soprano.
[8] See p. 59.
[9] Strauss had left the Festival in Graz early owing to the death of his father.
[10] Probably Richard Mayr (1877–1935), bass, at the Vienna Opera since 1902.
[11] Mahler composed his Seventh Symphony in the summers of 1904 and 1905.

Mahler to Strauss

Maiernigg
19 August 1905

Dear Friend

The notice has obviously been conjured from nowhere. The date of the première cannot possibly be decided yet.—All that is certain is that if I do not bring out your opera on 4 October,[1] it can probably not be performed until January. (December is excluded as too unfavourable for such an important new work, and because a new production of *Don Giovanni* must come out in November (the same for *Figaro* in December) for the Mozart jubilee.[)][2]

As soon as I reach Vienna I shall write to Fürstner.—Ill omens are once more coming from the censor.

Would you please, in any case, send the text *as soon as possible* (or the definitive version of Wilde's play) so that I can submit it to the censor[3] and, if need be, start brawling with him in good time. Also, the management will not approve a Kreuzer until the work has passed the censor.

I should like to start studying the work *at once*, as I intend to have three singers study Salome so as to have a choice and also a possible replacement.—*Kurz* is impossible. A wonderful voice, but impossible as an actress even for Lucia.—But I have high hopes of a slender young singer of colossal power and unfaltering high register, with whom I am starting to study the part at once. (Frl. *Bland*).[4] The rest of the cast fits my plans very well. *Schmedes*, *Mildenburg* and *Weidemann* (perhaps Demuth).

Narraboth I must think more about—but under no circumstances Slezak, who takes no trouble, sings in a slovenly, unrhythmical way, and gets off by the third performance. He must keep to Troubadour and Arnold.[5]

My Seventh is finished.—How did you get on this summer? Did you manage to get anything done apart from *Salome*?—Your *Feursnot* was capital,—but the jewel in the crown (Weidemann) was unfortunately missing.[6]—However, *Diemuth* was wonderful.[7]

Best wishes to you and your wife from us both.

I am just leaving for Vienna—alas!

Your most devoted friend
Gustav Mahler

[1] Name-day of the Emperor Franz Joseph, traditional date for premières.
[2] Mozart's 150th birthday in 1906.
[3] On 20 September 1905 Mahler was informed that the censorship office of the Court Theatres had 'for religious and moral reasons declared itself opposed to the acceptance of the libretto of the opera *Salome*'.
[4] Elsa Bland (1880–1935), soprano, guest performance at the Vienna Opera in 1905, appointed in 1906.
[5] Presumably the tenor roles of Manrico in Verdi's *Il Trovatore* and Arnold in Rossini's *Guillaume Tell*.
[6] He was ill.
[7] The role was sung by Gertrude Förstel.

Mahler to Strauss

IMPERIAL AND ROYAL COURT OPERA[1]
VIENNA
22 September 1905
[letter drafted but not sent]

Sir

According to a communication received by the Office of the Director of the Imperial and Royal Court Opera, the Censorship here has declared itself opposed 'for religious and moral reasons' to the acceptance of the libretto of the opera *Salome*, and 'the General Intendant of the Imperial

Correspondence 1888–1911

and Royal Court Theatre is thus not in a position to permit the performance of this dramatic work'.

I beg leave to inform you of this decision, and must regretfully abstain, under these circumstances, from producing your work.

I remain, Sir,

Yours faithfully
Mahler

[1] The original (official letter with Mahler's signature) is in the Haus-, Hof- und Staatsarchiv, Vienna, Hof-Operntheater, No. 1019/1905. Mahler did not send this letter off; it is still among his documents. Instead, as we may suppose from a telegram draft of the same day, he sent Strauss the following telegram: 'Please send 2 or 3 vocal scores of *Salome* as soon as possible, so that the main singers can begin studying their parts. Which firm is publishing the work? Regards, Mahler.' Mahler seems at this time to have intentionally avoided informing Strauss of the rejection by the censor. See the following letter from Strauss.

On 8 October 1905 Rainer Simons, Director of the second Viennese opera house, the Kaiser Jubiläums-Stadttheater und Volksoper, wrote the following letter to Richard Strauss in Berlin:

Dear Herr Kapellmeister

As I have just heard, your work *Salome* will not pass the censorship of the Court Opera. Would you be kind enough to let me know whether you are now willing to let me have the work.

Yours very sincerely
Simons

Strauss wrote a few lines below this inquiry and sent it to Mahler:

Strauss to Mahler

Berlin
10 October 1905[1]

Dear Friend

Is this true? Please return this letter. The Dresden première,[2] where the work has no censorship difficulties to overcome, is at the end of November!

Cordial regards
Rich. Strauss

Correspondence 1888–1911

[1] Original in the Strauss-Archiv, Garmisch-Partenkirchen.
[2] The Dresden première took place on 9 December 1905.

Mahler to Strauss

Vienna
11 October 1905

Dear Friend

It is the melancholy truth. Indeed: the *censor* has *already refused* it. So far no one knows about it, for I shall move Heaven and Earth to have this *bêtise* reversed. As yet I have not been able to trace whose influence is behind the ban.

This letter suits my purpose *very well*! *Salome* is, of course, *quite impossible* at the Jubiläumstheater.—But my plan is now to present such a performance *as possible*.—You must if necessary support me in this and even *pretend* to be negotiating for it.—I dare say that with this pistol to his head even our omniscient censor will be willing to talk to us. You would not believe what unpleasantness I have had to put up with from that quarter— as soon as I got back from Strasbourg,[1] when I spoke enthusiastically about the project.

It is only *for this reason* that I have been aiming at January—or even February—for *Salome*. I wanted to spare you this worry so as not to spoil your pleasure in the première. Apart from that I hoped, and still hope, that the fact that as Catholic a Court as Dresden allows the performance will carry weight here.—So, please—keep *silent* for a while; write to *Simon*[s] that if the Court Opera refuses, a performance at the Jubiläumstheater will be considered. I ask you to let me keep the letter for a few more days. I hope it may serve me as an (unlooked-for) weapon in the unequal struggle.

And now, dear Strauss—I cannot help speaking of the moving impression your work made on me when I read it recently! This is your apogee so far! Indeed, I assert that *nothing* that even you have done up to now can be compared to it.—You know—I don't go in for empty phrases. With you even less than with others. Every note is right! What I have long known: you are a natural dramatist! I confess that it is only through your music that Wilde's work has become comprehensible to me. I hope to be able to attend the première in Dresden.—Let me know whether you consent to my plan of campaign. You have my word that I shall leave no stone unturned and shall never flag in championing this incomparable, thoroughly original masterpiece.

In great haste
Yours most sincerely
Gustav Mahler

[1] Strauss had played *Salome* to Mahler on the piano in Strasbourg (see p. 136).

Mahler to Strauss

The Director
Imp. and Royal Court Opera
[mid-October 1905]

Dear Friend,—In great haste! I am now somewhat more hopeful. This letter has done me very *good service*.[1] I hope to be able to let you have definite news in the next few days.—Please excuse the desolate state of the enclosed letter. I tore it up by mistake and had to retrieve the pieces from the waste-paper basket.

Sincerely
Mahler

[1] The letter from Rainer Simons to Strauss, see the previous exchange of letters between Mahler and Strauss.

Mahler to Strauss

The Director
Imp. and Royal Court Opera
[22 or 23 October 1905]

In haste!

My dear Friend—at last I have something *gratifying* to report! The *difficulties* are removed! Your *Salome* has been passed! I have just been to the censor. Within a week he will return the libretto to me with passages marked where he would like *the expression* modified a little. I have his promise that nothing *fundamental* needs to be changed.—

Unfortunately, he objects to the name *Jochanaan*. He requires it changed. I suggested Bal Hanaan. However, if you have a different wish, please let me know by return.—Once I have his comments I shall send them to you (perhaps with my suggestions), and we shall get down to studying the work at once. I am going to cast *Salome* four times (as I have no female who *completely* matches my conception of the part) and you can then choose the one that you think most suited. It is of the utmost importance to me that the performer's *voice* and *singing ability* should meet your demands, so that I cannot propose Schoder.[1] What do you think? The rest of the cast is as we agreed. With cordial regards, and a sigh of relief,

Mahler

---

[1] Marie Gutheil Schoder, famous as much for her acting as her singing, was clearly ideal for the part in Mahler's eyes, but he knew that Strauss did not accept her type of singer. Strauss later became one of her admirers and she sang Octavian in the Vienna première of *Rosenkavalier* (1911).

Strauss to Mahler

24 October 1905[1]

Dear Friend

Thank you for the happy news of yesterday, and above all for your unselfish efforts, and not less for your (and your wife's) kind letter of condolence recently. The recognition you accord my work, words that one hears so seldom from colleagues and that one really needs so much, gave me almost more pleasure than the news that your omniscient censor had withdrawn the ban. I agree, of course, to all the changes you wish. The changing of John's name, whose story[2] every schoolboy knows, is delightful.

In Dresden, as prima donna Wittich condescended too late to learn her part, the first performance has had to be postponed until December. I yesterday gave Schuch 9 December as the last date for which I can guarantee him the first performance. If he has not brought the work out by then, those who can steal a march on him are free to do so. So you have a clear run. I would mention that on the evening of 13 December I am leaving for Warsaw, Moscow and St. Petersburg, and shall only return at the beginning of [January? illegible].

Now you can arrange things as you think fit. Do you wish to have your performance immediately after the Dresden one, say on 12 December? Or postpone it until January?

The score is already engraved; the orchestral parts will be ready by 10 November.

You already have a celesta; you need only get a heckelphone!

Thank you again (and your dear wife), and please accept my warmest good wishes (from my wife also).

Yours very sincerely
Dr Richard Strauss

---

[1] Transcript by Alma Mahler.
[2] Strauss's pun (*halsbrecherische Geschichte*, literally 'neckbreaking story') is untranslatable.

Mahler to Strauss

The Director
Imp. and Royal Court Opera
[31 October 1905]

Dear Friend

My bulletin for today is, alas, somewhat less cheerful. These accursed newspaper hacks (heaven knows who they got the story from—I told no one) have completely spoiled things again. The censor, who had definitely agreed to the performance—he merely required *textual* changes of which he would notify me within a week—must have been worked on by someone in the meantime. For he has just returned the text to me with a long disquisition (I shall bring the letter with me to Berlin, where I shall be on *7th and 8th*) and speaks again of 'the depiction of acts that belong to the sphere of sexual pathology and are not suited to our stage'.[1] That confounded escape into *generalities* all over again, against which there are no weapons! *I beg you, dear Strauss*—keep *everything between ourselves from now on*, otherwise we shall get hopelessly stuck. On Tuesday I shall see him in person and take the bull by the horns. *I shall not give in*, and regard your *Salome* as my own personal affair. What damages me most here is the damned postponement in Dresden, which is interpreted here in 'influential quarters' as a sign of censorship difficulties there. The devil knows where this wind is blowing from.—Please let me know where and when we can talk things over *thoroughly* in Berlin on the days mentioned (in the afternoon—or evening of the 7th we have the final rehearsal—the concert is on the evening of the 8th;[2] *otherwise* I am entirely at your disposal!).

Best wishes
Yours sincerely
Mahler

[1] Quotation from the censor's letter to Mahler of 31 October.
[2] On 8 November 1905 Oscar Fried conducted a performance of Mahler's Second Symphony in Berlin.

Strauss to Mahler

Berlin
1 November 1905[1]

Dear Friend

Thank you for your kind letter; I spoke to Schuch yesterday: the Dresden première has been postponed by a week, from 28 November to 8 December,[2] for the simple reason that the orchestral parts are not yet ready and cannot be sent to Dresden before mid-November.—Schuch told me in confidence that the Vienna Censor Dr Jellinek[3] had asked him whether *Salome* had met with censorship difficulties in Dresden. Schuch answered: not the slightest. I hope this reassured the Vienna censor.

So you are coming on 7 November? I am here and ask you simply to decide when you would like to speak to me, and when you would like to dine with me. I am completely free on 7 and 8 November. My telephone number is: Charlottenburg 1145.

Looking forward to meeting you, and a thousand thanks for everything!

Yours
Dr Richard Strauss

[1] Transcript by Alma Mahler.
[2] The Dresden première in fact took place on 9 December.
[3] Strauss probably means Hofrat Dr Emil Jettel von Ettenach.

Correspondence 1888–1911

Strauss to Mahler

Berlin
15 December 1905[1]

Dear Friend

Where were you on the 9th?[2] I missed you *very* much.

You missed a magnificent performance: Schuch's and Burrian's[3] achievement was quite extraordinary. You really ought to see the Dresden performance: you would enjoy it.

The first three performances were completely sold out: the orchestra indescribably beautiful.

How do things stand in Vienna? I am waiting impatiently for favourable news from you. Who is to perform this horribly difficult work if the theatres that really can play it fail to do so?

Best regards from us to you both,

Yours
Dr Richard Strauss

[1] Transcript by Alma Mahler.
[2] The day of the first performance of *Salome* in Dresden.
[3] Karl Burrian (1870–1924) sang Herod in Dresden.

Mahler to Strauss

The Director
Imp. and Royal Court Opera
[winter of 1905–6]

Dear Friend

Your letter comes at a very opportune moment. The situation for your affairs *is good*! (Please, *only* between ourselves, otherwise I can answer for nothing.) Nevertheless, I still need help.—The *censor* has already changed his mind and is not presenting the slightest obstacle. But *higher* up there is still a barrier to be broken down.[1] Curiously, I was chipping at it only *yesterday*. Your letter is *very* helpful to my purpose. Please, keep on negotiating quite casually with Simons.

But I assure you, in the *autumn* we shall have *Salome*! (It is, of course, quite impossible at the Jubiläumstheater)—I keep trying to go to Dresden for a performance and something always prevents me. In spring I am sure

Correspondence 1888–1911

to attend one—I should be delighted if you could be there too. In any case I shall let you know in good time.

Sincerely yours
Mahler

[1] The prohibition of *Salome* at the Vienna Court Opera is said to have been instigated by an archduchess.

Strauss to Mahler

22 December 1905[1]

Can you send me a Diemut[2] for 2 performances Feuersnot in Munich 28 December? Please wire immediately stating fee. Strauss Hotel 4 Seasons.

[1] The transcript of this telegram is in the Strauss-Archiv, Garmisch-Partenkirchen.
[2] One of the principal soprano roles in *Feuersnot*, properly spelt Diemuth.

Mahler to Strauss

The Director
Imp. and Royal Court Opera
[22 or 23 December 1905]

Dear Friend

From the telegram now being sent you will see that *Förstel*[1] is only available after 7 January. Can you still use her then?—She is delightful.—I shall, of course, put Michalek at your disposal and will see to it that she rehearses the part immediately![2] When would you like her to be in Munich? I am in hot pursuit of *Salome* whenever the slightest chance presents itself. *I shall get my way*, you may depend on that. But you must have patience. The situation being as it is, I shall hardly manage it before the *autumn* of 1906. The goings-on here are a disgrace. I am terribly sorry I cannot perform this glorious work *at once*. But you will enjoy it when the time comes.

A thousand greetings
Yours
Mahler

Correspondence 1888–1911

[1] Gertrude Förstel sang Diemuth in the new performance of *Feuersnot* in June 1905.
[2] Margarete Michalek (1875–?) sang Diemuth at the Vienna first performance in January 1902. Neither Förstel nor Michalek sang in Munich, as Strauss cabled on 23 December that he had a replacement from Dresden.

Mahler to Strauss

The Director
Imp. and Royal Court Opera
[mid-March 1906]

Dear Friend

I cannot prevent the Breslau enterprise[1] and would not wish to. It might well be the best way to bring my opponents to their senses.—You would not believe how vexatious this matter has been for me or (between ourselves) what consequences it may have for me.

For—I give you my word—I shall not give in even if it should involve a 'question of confidence'.[2] If the Breslau people have the courage, then God be with them! I would place myself entirely at Herr Löwe's[3] disposal—should he need our *musicians* or anything else, and *Roller*[4] would give him any support needed with scenery.

With sincere regards
Yours
Mahler

I have just heard a splendid performance in *Amsterdam* of your *Taillefer*, of which I am *especially* fond among your works.[5]

[1] The United Theatres of Breslau were planning a tour with *Salome*, including performances in Vienna.
[2] The ban on *Salome* was not the reason for Mahler's resignation in 1907, but undoubtedly influenced his decision (see pp. 138f.).
[3] Dr Theodor Löwe, Director of the United Theatres in Breslau.
[4] Alfred Roller (1864–1935), painter appointed by Mahler as scenery manager at the Court Opera in 1903.
[5] On 10 March 1906 Mahler conducted *Das klagende Lied* at the Concertgebouw, while Willem Mengelberg conducted *Taillefer*, Op. 52, by Strauss in the same concert series.

Correspondence 1888–1911

Strauss to Mahler

Berlin W. 15
15 March 1906[1]

Dear Friend

As you have so kindly agreed that a Breslau performance in Vienna seems likely to further our cause, I today conveyed my assent to Herr Dr Löwe and let him know you are willing to support him so magnanimously, for which he is extremely grateful. Let us hope that this will not now rebound against us by blocking *Salome*'s way to the Court Opera instead of smoothing it. Löwe intends to bring the entire orchestra from Breslau, but thankfully accepts the help of the inspired Roller with sets and costumes.

I was very reluctant to agree, as I am loath to deprive you of the Vienna first performance; but after the enormous struggles you have had, a great success for the Breslau *Salome* in Vienna seems almost the only possible way of preventing influential court circles from blocking *Salome*'s adoption by the Court Opera.

I hope you are not inwardly displeased with me over this; if that were the case, I should withdraw my permission today;[2] and for heaven's sake do not let *Salome* give rise to a question of confidence! We need an artist of your determination, your genius and your outlook in such a position too badly for you to put anything at stake on *Salome*'s account. In the end we shall attain our ends without this!

Thank you again for everything, and best wishes to you and your dear wife,

Ever yours
Richard Strauss

---

[1] Transcript by Alma Mahler.
[2] The invitation performances by the Breslau United Theatres did not take place in Vienna in spring 1906, but only from 25 May to 20 June 1907. It is not known whether the delay was for practical reasons or was occasioned by Strauss.

Correspondence 1888–1911

Strauss to Mahler

Marquartstein
Upper Bavaria
7 June 1906[1]

Dear Friend

Fürstner is prepared to dedicate a *Salome* score[2] to you for your private library, if you are willing to sign a declaration obliging your heirs to return the score to me on your decease.

If you agree, the score will be sent to you at once. Was the Sixth[3] to your liking?

Will you soon be able to send me good news about *Salome* in Vienna?

Best wishes to you both
Yours ever
Richard Strauss

---

[1] Transcript by Alma Mahler.

[2] As the Vienna Court Opera had not concluded an agreement to perform the work, Mahler knew it only from the vocal score and from a performance in Graz in May 1906.

[3] The first performance of Mahler's Sixth Symphony was in Essen on 27 May 1906 at the Festival of the Allgemeiner Deutscher Musikverein (see pp. 141 ff.).

Mahler to Strauss

The Director
Imp. and Royal Court Opera
[between 8 and 10 June 1906]

Dear Friend

I am willing, of course, to sign the declaration. He should just send the score at once, for I have a great desire to lose myself in the mysterious labyrinth.—I had a talk with an influential person concerning *Salome* as soon as I got back here.[1] If I have not yet secured their agreement, I can report a promising 'indecision'. (I did not expect anything more to begin with.) I also mentioned your readiness to grant me an extension until 1 November, which was accepted with significant alacrity.—All in all I think I can count with certainty on being able to *perform Salome next year*.—A definitive answer in the autumn, if this is agreeable to you.—I am beginning to recover my spirits. No doubt all this must be.

Yours sincerely
Mahler

[1] From the Festival in Essen.

Mahler to Strauss

The Director
Imp. and Royal Court Opera
[October 1906?][1]

Dear Friend

Reluctant as I am, I must tell you as early as possible: *permission is still withheld*! My objection that I must *decide* by 1 November is answered with a shrug.—Now I should welcome it if *Löwe* could put on a performance here as soon as possible. That would breach their defences.

It is *too stupid*!

This in haste for your information. I hope to see you in Berlin on 8 November.

Yours most sincerely
Mahler

[1] The date of this letter cannot be determined unequivocally. The content suggests late September/early October 1906; but the mention of 8 November makes October 1905 seem likely. On 8 November 1905 Mahler's Second Symphony was performed in his presence in Berlin (see p. 89). Possibly, as often happened with dates, Mahler has made a slip of the pen and means 8 October. This would refer to 8 October 1906, when his Sixth Symphony was performed in Mahler's presence in Berlin (under Oscar Fried).

Correspondence 1888–1911

Strauss to Mahler

Berlin
14 January 1907[1]

Dear Friend

I have to conduct external concerts every evening for the whole week including Saturday and, urgently in need of rest, must forgo hearing your magnificent work[2] once more this evening. The first movements, that I heard yesterday, again made the deepest impression on me in their particular strength and freshness of invention, and I was sincerely glad to see how the audience is beginning to love and understand your art.

I wrote to Fürstner again today and hope you will soon be able to call the *Salome* score your own. As soon as Fürstner is well again, I hope to settle the matter finally. I am sure you will not attribute my absence today to a lack of interest or admiration, but to my over-exertion in the past weeks.

Please give your wife our regards, and accept our best wishes,

Your devoted friend
Dr Richard Strauss

[1] Postcard transcribed by Alma Mahler.
[2] The Third Symphony, performed at a Berlin Philharmonic Concert on 14 January 1907 under Mahler.

Mahler to Strauss

The Director
Imp. and Royal Court Opera
[6 February 1907]

Dear Friend

I heard the new *Schoenberg* quartet[1] yesterday and found it so profound and impressive that I cannot but recommend it most emphatically for the Dresden Festival. I enclose the score and hope you will have time to look at it.—The *Rosé* Quartet[2] offers to interpret it if their *travelling expenses are paid*.

Forgive me for pestering you, but I think you will have much pleasure from this.

Yours sincerely and in haste
Mahler

1 Mahler waiting for Strauss at the door of the Landestheater, Salzburg, 1906.

2 Gustav Mahler, 1907.    3 Richard Strauss, 1907.

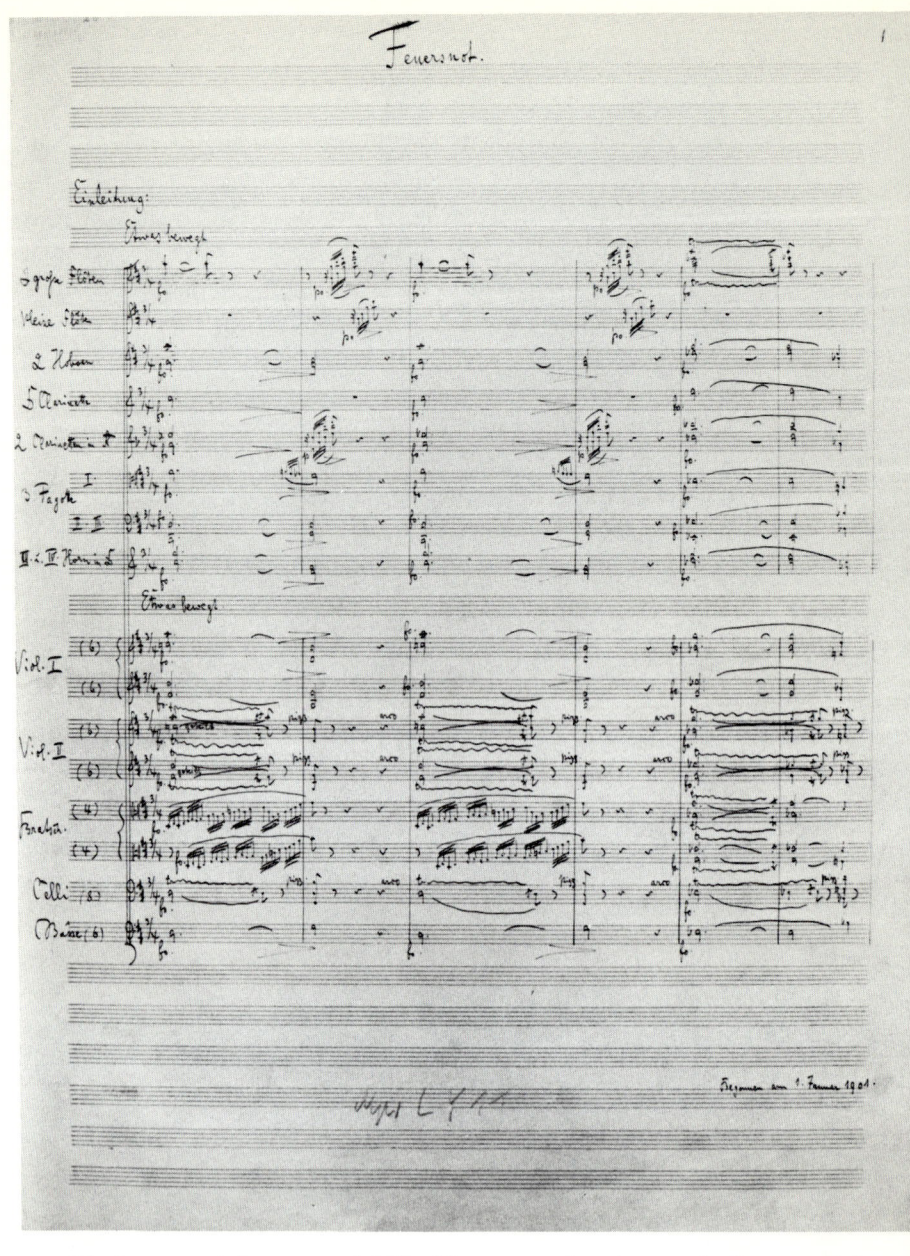

4   The first page of the autograph MS of Feuersnot, *the only opera by Strauss which Mahler conducted.*

5   *The first page of the autograph of Mahler's Fourth Symphony, a work which Strauss especially valued.*

6 *The Strauss family.*

7 *Alma and Gustav Mahler, about 1903.*

TEATRO COLON

Concesionarios: Empresa:
FAUSTINO DA ROSA - WALTER MOCCHI   WALTER MOCCHI y Cía.

MARTES 14 DE AGOSTO

A las 21.15

SEGUNDO CONCIERTO DE ABONO

a MARTES y VIERNES

POR LA

FILARMONICA DE VIENA

bajo la dirección del maestro

RICARDO STRAUSS

PROGRAMA

I.

1ra. Sinfonía en re mayor . . . . **MALHER**
    Lento
    Muy agitato
    Solemne e moderato
    Muy agitato

II.

Obertura Coriolano . . . . **BEETHOVEN**
Concierto en mi bemol para piano y orquesta . . **BEETHOVEN**
    Allegro
    Adagio. — Un poco mosso. — Rondo
    Allegro ma non troppo
Al piano: Señor ALFRED BLUMEN

III.

Muerte y Transfiguración. (Escena Sinfónica) . . **STRAUSS**

NOTA. — Durante la ejecución de las obras, no se permitirá la entrada a la platea.

8 Announcement of Strauss's performance of Mahler's First Symphony with the Vienna Philharmonic Orchestra, Buenos Aires, 1923.

9 Facsimile of Mahler's letter to Strauss, 19 August 1905, see p. 82.

10 *Facsimile of Strauss's letter to Mahler, June 1901, see p. 52*

Vereinigung schaffender Tonkünstler in Wien.

Mittwoch den 23. November 1904, abends halb 8 Uhr
im Großen Musikvereinssaale

I. Orchesterkonzert.

Mitwirkend:

Direktor Gustav **Mahler** (Ehrenpräsident).　　Hermann **Bischoff** (auswärtiges Mitglied).
Kapellmeister Alexander v. **Zemlinszky**　　K. k. Hofopernsänger Friedrich **Weidemann**.
(ordentliches Mitglied).　　Das Orchester des Wiener Konzertvereines.

Programm:

1. Siegmund v. Hausegger: Dionysische Phantasie.
   Dirigent: Alexander v. Zemlinszky.
2. Hermann Bischoff: Drei Gesänge mit Orchester.
   a) Das Trinklied.
   b) Der Schlaf.
   c) Bewegte See.
   K. k. Hofopernsänger Friedrich Weidemann. — Dirigent: Der Komponist.
3. Richard Strauss: Symphonia domestica. Dirigent: Gustav Mahler.

I. Kammermusik- und Liederabend	II. Orchesterkonzert	II. Kammermusik- u. Liederabend
20. Dezember 1904, halb 8 Uhr abends im Saale Bösendorfer.	25. Jänner 1905, halb 8 Uhr abends im Großen Musikvereinssaale.	20. Jänner 1905, halb 8 Uhr abends im Saale Bösendorfer.
1. Gerhard v. Keussler: Gesänge.	1. Alexander v. Zemlinszky: Die Seejungfrau. Phantasie für Orchester.	Ein Liederabend mit Orchester 29. Jänner 1905, halb 8 Uhr abends im Kleinen Musikvereinssaale. Zur Aufführung gelangen ausschließlich Lieder von Gustav Mahler.
2. Hans Pfitzner: Klaviertrio F dur.	2. Oskar C. Posa: Fünf Gedichte von Detlev v. Liliencron für Bariton mit Orchester.	III. Kammermusik- u. Liederabend 20. Februar 1905, halb 8 Uhr abends im Saale Bösendorfer.
3. Rudolf St. Hoffmann: Gesänge.	3. Arnold Schönberg: Pelleas und Melisande, symphonische Dichtung.	III. Orchesterkonzert 11. März 1905, halb 8 Uhr abends im Großen Musikvereinssaale.
4. Kurt Schindler: Gesänge.		

Programme à 20 Heller.

11　Announcement of Mahler's performance of Strauss's Symphonia domestica, *Vienna, 23 November 1904.*

Correspondence 1888–1911

Many thanks for *Salome*.
It simply will not leave my desk.

[1] String Quartet in D minor, Op. 7 by Arnold Schoenberg (1874–1951), first performed on 5 February 1907 in Vienna.
[2] The quartet led by Mahler's brother-in-law Arnold Rosé (1863–1946).

Mahler to Strauss

The Director
Imp. and Royal Court Opera
[May 1907?][1]

Dear Friend

I am sure you will know what is going on here. I'm leaving.—A consequence that I can predict with certainty is, unfortunately, that *Roller*, that outstanding artist and practitioner of rare talent, will not be able to stay.[2]—This affects me greatly, as it seems to me of utmost importance to keep him for the theatre. There are possibilities in him that no one can yet suspect.

It occurs to me that perhaps Berlin (above all, you in Berlin) can make use of him! You can expect remarkable things of him! I pass this idea on to you in case something may come of it.[3]—But please treat it with strictest confidentiality, as it could be badly misunderstood here.—Could you send me a few lines to let me know how I should advise him? In haste,

Yours very sincerely
Mahler

[1] The exact date of Mahler's resignation is not known, though negotiations apparently went on throughout May 1907.
[2] Roller remained scenery manager at the Court Opera until 31 May 1909. Strauss had a long conversation with Roller (see letter of Alfred Roller to Gustav Mahler, 11 March 1908, *AM* pp. 313–6). For the first performance of *Rosenkavalier* (Dresden, 26 January 1911) Roller created scenery and costumes that remained exemplary for decades.

Correspondence 1888-1911

Mahler to Strauss

[Vienna]
[May/June 1909]

Dear Friend

By a somewhat roundabout route via New York[1] and Paris I have received your card.

As far as I know, my First lasts about 50 minutes.[2] I have not yet any plans for the summer. In a few days I am going by rail to Toblach in the *Tyrol*. Burying myself there for a while. It is too bad that it is so far from you, otherwise I should certainly descend on you. Unfortunately, I have not yet heard your *Elektra*! I cannot go to the theatre here (Weingartner would have me ejected by the police) so I must wait until I hear it in New York.—Your *Salome* was given a very *vulgar* performance,[3] but owing to a *wonderful* interpretation of the title role by Mary Garden[4] made a *powerful impression*. Dalmorès as Herodes is capital as well![5]

Best wishes to you and your wife from us both.

Yours ever
Mahler

[1] Since his resignation as Director of the Vienna Opera, Mahler had been conducting in New York, but spent most of the year in Europe.
[2] Strauss performed Mahler's First Symphony at a concert by the Royal Orchestra in Berlin on 3 December 1909.
[3] At the Manhattan Opera House in New York.
[4] Mary Garden (1877–1967), soprano.
[5] Charles Dalmorès (1871–1939), tenor.

Strauss to Mahler

Garmisch
21 August 1909[1]

Dear Friend

On Monday morning we leave for a nine-day automobile tour of the Dolomites and hope to come to Toblach and see you on Monday evening or Tuesday.[2]

The barometer is falling, but the weather on the other side of the Brenner is always different to ours. Would you be so very kind as to send me a telegram tomorrow, Sunday evening: (Strauss Garmisch), to say whether the weather is fine where you are and is likely to last.

Hoping to see you soon!

Best wishes from us both to you both
Yours
Dr Richard Strauss

[1] Transcript by Alma Mahler.
[2] The visit of the Strauss family to Mahler in Toblach did take place.

Mahler to Strauss

[late September 1909]

My dear Friend

One request: please send me a postcard with the address of the Paris manuscript paper firm.[1] — My summer was very good,[2] and you will once again be in the rococo.[3] What a pity our 'interview' was so short,[4] almost as between potentates. — I am conducting my Seventh at the beginning of October in Amsterdam. Please send your reply there: Concertgebouw.

Best wishes from your old friend
Gustav Mahler

[1] At that time Strauss was writing his scores on paper supplied by the Papeterie de Leysse près Chambery-Forest (watermark), H. Lardesnault/Ed. Bellamy Sr/ Paris (stamp).
[2] In the summer of 1909 Mahler composed his Ninth Symphony.
[3] Allusion to *Rosenkavalier* on which Strauss was working.
[4] The meeting at Toblach mentioned in Strauss's previous letter.

Correspondence 1888–1911

Strauss to Mahler

Landhaus Richard Strauss
Garmisch
11 May 1911[1]

Dear Friend

I read with great pleasure that you are feeling better and are recovering from your long illness.[2] Perhaps it may be some diversion in the melancholy hours of convalescence to know that next winter, probably in early December, I shall perform with the Royal Orchestra in Berlin: your Third Symphony. If you would like to conduct yourself (you will be pleased with the orchestra), it will be a pleasure to hear your lovely work under your own direction again, much as I should like, of course, to conduct it myself. I should naturally rehearse it in any case, so that you will have no trouble, only enjoyment.

With the heartfelt wish that you may have completely recovered soon, and with very best wishes from my wife too, who follows the news of your condition with deepest sympathy,

Most sincerely and respectfully yours
Richard Strauss

Best regards to your wife, your mother-in-law and your sister.

---

[1] The autograph of this letter is in the Alma Mahler-Werfel Bequest, University of Pennsylvania.

[2] Mahler fell critically ill in February 1911 in New York and was transported to Vienna via Paris. He died on 18 May 1911.

[3] Strauss conducted Mahler's work at the concert on 11 December 1911 in Berlin.

RIVALRY
AND FRIENDSHIP

Rivalry and Friendship

An Essay on the Mahler–Strauss Relationship
by Herta Blaukopf

About seventy years after Mahler's death, and some thirty after Strauss's, we now present the correspondence in which their friendship was recorded. A conspicuous delay. The more so if we remember that Strauss and Mahler knew each other for twenty-four years, spent long hours and sometimes days in discussion and were also linked by many practical concerns. While the documents reflecting the relationship between Strauss and Mahler remained unpublished, knowledge of what they had in common was gradually lost.

As early as 1924 Alma Mahler published a volume of letters by her deceased husband.[1] This volume, containing a total of 420 letters by Mahler to friends and colleagues, does not print a single one of the many letters which Mahler addressed to Strauss. Even more surprising, there is no indication that such letters exist. Now it is conceivable that Alma Mahler, always ill-disposed towards Strauss, omitted the letters intentionally, but it is no less plausible that Strauss, as the owner of the letters, refused to have them published in 1924. This, too, is a mere supposition, but one that is reinforced by Strauss's refusal in 1939, when Alma Mahler sought permission to print a number of letters addressed by Strauss to Mahler. So it came about that these two important collections of correspondence[2] contain neither letters from Mahler to Strauss nor letters from Strauss to Mahler.

After the Second World War isolated letters by Mahler to Strauss appear in the Strauss literature—in biographies, exhibitions and exhibition catalogues, and in published selections such as *Die Welt um Richard Strauss in Briefen*.[3] But none of these went beyond individual publications that could

Rivalry and Friendship

not reflect either the extent of the correspondence or the relationship between the two composers. A comprehensive publication was not attempted, as the whereabouts of the letters written by Strauss to Mahler was unknown. Whereas Mahler's letters to Strauss are kept almost without exception in the archive of his heirs in Garmisch-Partenkirchen, Strauss's letters to Mahler were never collected and preserved. Even for this edition, despite years of searching, only some of the letters originally written have been located. Thus, as opposed to the sixty-three letters by Mahler published here, there are only twenty-eight by Strauss, and of these a dozen have been preserved only in transcripts by Alma Mahler. The originals disappeared, probably with a number of other documents from Mahler's legacy, during the air raids on Vienna in 1945.

Mahler appears always to have been rather careless with letters sent to him, and to have thrown many away. Only this can explain why so few letters addressed to him have come to light in public and private collections, in auction houses, and among dealers. After her husband's death Alma Mahler discovered a portfolio containing documents from the years 1880 to 1886, including letters from his parents and brothers and sisters.[4] This is the only collection of this kind known to us. Whether there were similar portfolios from later years is not known. However, Mahler's sisters Justine and Emma kept a number of letters addressed to him whose writers seemed interesting to them, and in this way, with letters by Pietro Mascagni and Anton Bruckner, some by Strauss have survived. But these are only isolated fragments. The great majority of all letters addressed to Mahler—and their number can be estimated from his replies—must be regarded as lost. Alma Mahler, it is true, published a number of letters to Mahler from the period 1904–10, in her memoirs,[5] but these few pieces look like chance discoveries rather than a considered selection from an abundant correspondence archive. The twelve letters from Strauss that Alma originally wanted to incorporate in her book on Mahler and that probably survive only in her transcripts, likewise have this random character about them. To sum up, it can be said that even from the years of Mahler's marriage no letters to him have turned up, not even letters from his wife, and without these some of his own remain incomprehensible.

Those contemporaries who knew Gustav Mahler and Richard Strauss personally often mentioned them in the same breath, yet they were also

Rivalry and Friendship

generally seen as radically opposed: antithetical in their musical means and goals as in their temperaments and personalities. Ludwig Schiedermair, who knew both composers in Munich before the turn of the century, characterized their diverging natures as follows: 'Richard Strauss, the productive artist deliberately pursuing his goal and keeping his feet on firm ground however high he aspired—Gustav Mahler, consumed by his artistic intensity, struggling restlessly towards the loftiest goals....'[6]

Mahler himself was aware, only too aware, of the traits of character that distinguished him from Strauss, and emphasized them on many occasions. In a letter to the music critic Arthur Seidl in 1897 (see p. 122) he described his relationship to Strauss in terms of Schopenhauer's image of two miners tunnelling from opposite directions, who eventually meet.[7] According to Alma Mahler's memoirs Mahler also used this image in conversation in later years. 'Mahler used to say,' she writes, 'that Strauss and I are digging our tunnels from different sides of the same mountain. We shall surely meet some day.'[8]

No comparable statement by Strauss has been recorded. To him Mahler was a colleague, perhaps even a friend, whose achievements as a composer and conductor he acknowledged; but his relationship to Mahler was not burdened with psychological problems.

The curious metaphor of the mountain chosen by Mahler, which expresses his ambivalent attitude to Strauss, undoubtedly did not come to him by chance. He felt that between himself and his colleague there was a mountain blocking the view each had of the other, a climatic barrier that was conditioned by a fundamental difference of being. 'Mahler and Strauss enjoyed each other's conversation, perhaps because they were never of the same opinion,' Alma Mahler records.[9] However, the antithesis was overlaid by much common ground. When they first met in 1887 they were both under the spell of Richard Wagner, who was still a controversial figure. Both were composing and knew enough of their craft to see before long that it was they—Strauss and Mahler—who were to show music the way after Wagner. Both earned their livings as orchestral conductors, both suffered under the inadequacies of the theatre business. If Mahler and Strauss took such different directions as composers despite their common experience of Wagner, they nevertheless felt that they were partners.

By origin they were as unlike as night and day: one the son of a respected Munich musician, the other of a Jewish distiller from the Bohemian

Rivalry and Friendship

village of Kalište. In Strauss's home there were only two children, Richard and a younger sister, on whom parental love and attention were focused, while Mahler had thirteen siblings of whom eight died in childhood. Here a childhood darkened by poverty and death, there a happy one. Strauss was a good pupil. His cheerful temperament and lively mind made him a favourite with his teachers, who even turned a blind eye when he composed in lessons. Alongside the usual instrumental lessons he received instruction from colleagues of his father in harmony and counterpoint, and, while still at school, without having ever visited a conservatory, he made his bow before the Munich audience as a composer. When he was twenty, Hans von Bülow, the leading conductor of his time, accepted for performance the wind serenade, Op. 7, by the young Strauss. Mahler, too, received instrumental tuition in early childhood, but to become a musician he had to leave his parental home at fifteen and go with insufficient means to the conservatory at Vienna. He made ends meet by giving piano lessons while still at school himself. At twenty he composed *Das klagende Lied*, which remained in his drawer as a manuscript and was performed for the first time in 1901, when Mahler had long been Director of the Court Opera. If it is true that childhood and early youth stamp the human personality, the artist's above all, for life, it can be understood why Mahler developed into the harbinger of suffering who is known to us, and Strauss into the bestower of joy.

These deliberately simplified labels should not, of course, give the impression that Mahler's life was spent in renunciation and failure, while Strauss hastened from one easy conquest to the next. That was not the case. If Strauss got his works accepted more quickly, Mahler had an immense advantage as a conductor, for we find him installed as Director of the Royal Hungarian Opera House when Strauss had to be glad of a place as second conductor at Weimar.

The frequent journeys which are part of the conductor's profession brought Strauss and Mahler relatively often together, even though they never spent a long period in the same place. When they stayed for a few days in the same town, they spent a large part of their free time together. Between these personal meetings they exchanged letters. This connection was never broken off in the twenty-four years of their acquaintance, even though times of frequent meetings and numerous letters alternate with periods of sparser contacts. The presentation of their correspondence, as far as it has been preserved and is accessible, now makes it possible for the first time to reconstruct the personal relationship between Strauss and Mahler

Rivalry and Friendship

in its entirety. This attempt also makes use of all the other sources, apart from the letters, that are able to throw light on these artists' friendship.

In October 1887 Richard Strauss, at that time third conductor at the Munich Opera, came to Leipzig where for about a year Gustav Mahler had been second conductor at the Stadttheater. The occasion for the journey was the concert given by the Gewandhaus Orchestra on 13 October, at which Strauss conducted his F minor Symphony. How and through whom he made Mahler's acquaintance is not known. Max Steinitzer, whom Mahler met frequently in his Leipzig days, probably played a part, for many decades later Strauss wrote the following in his so-called 'Grey Diary': 'Max Steinitzer, my later biographer and a friend of my youth, had sung the praises of Mahler, who was a conductor in Leipzig and was arranging posthumous sketches of Weber's *Drei Pintos*.'[10]

If this recollection is correct, Steinitzer probably also introduced the two young conductors, the 27-year-old Mahler and the 23-year-old Strauss. We may suppose that Strauss's name was already familiar to Mahler, not only from Steinitzer's accounts but through the very frequent performances of his works, above all the F minor Symphony. This work, which according to Steinitzer contains 'a great deal of genuine Strauss' but 'still within the framework of strict form',[11] had had its first performance, by the New York Philharmonic Society, as early as December 1884; Franz Wüllner had conducted the German first performance in Cologne, which had been followed by renditions under Strauss in Meiningen, under Hermann Levi in Munich, under Robert Radecke in Berlin, under Jean Louis Nicodé in Dresden and under Hans von Bülow in Hamburg. Mahler must also have known that in the 1885–6 season Strauss had been Music Director under Bülow at the court of Meiningen, a position that Mahler himself had passionately desired. When he was underemployed and utterly dejected as Music Director in Kassel, he had heard Bülow conducting the Meiningen orchestra and had sent to him an extravagantly worded petition culminating in the words: 'When at yesterday's concert I saw fulfilled the loveliest thing I had dimly hoped for, it was clear to me: this is your homeland—this is your master—now your wandering shall end, or never! And now I am here and ask you: Take me with you—in whatever form—let me be your pupil, even if I must pay my fees in blood....'[12]

That had been written at the end of 1884, and Mahler had come far as a conductor since then, even without Bülow's help. But as a composer he had

Rivalry and Friendship

not yet made an appearance, if we disregard three songs that had been performed at a Prague concert [18 April 1886]. Indeed, for his years, especially if we compare him with the younger Strauss, he had produced surprisingly little. In 1887 Carl Maria von Weber's sketches for the comic opera *Die drei Pintos* came to Mahler's notice in Leipzig and he undertook to produce, from these scanty fragments and other music by Weber, a stage version that could be performed. Naturally there was not only a lot of harmonizing and instrumentation to be done, there were parts to be completed and even to be composed, but for reasons of expediency Mahler had to hide behind Weber. It was a piece of restoration that gave Mahler much pleasure, but it was not work in which his own personality could be fully expressed.

On 29 October 1887, soon after his return to Munich, Strauss sent Hans von Bülow a report on his stay at Leipzig, in which he spoke at length of Mahler.

> I made a new, very delightful acquaintance in Herr Mahler, who seemed to me a highly intelligent musician and conductor; one of the few modern conductors who knows about tempo modification, and in general had excellent views, particularly on Wagner's tempi (contrary to those of the now accredited Wagner conductors).
>
> Mahler's arrangement of Weber's *Drei Pintos* seems to me a masterpiece; the first act, which Mahler played to me, I found quite delightful ... I think you will also enjoy it![13]

On this enthusiastic recommendation Bülow studied the vocal score and, undeterred by the success of the Leipzig première of the *Drei Pintos*, condemned it utterly. In a letter of 27 March 1888 he reprimanded Strauss vigorously, accusing him of 'acute lack of judgement' and declaring that with the best will it was impossible to find anything praiseworthy in the work: 'No matter whether it Weberizes or Mahlerizes—by Jove it makes no difference—the whole thing is infamous, antiquated rubbish.'[14]

In face of this rejection by the conductor who, in his eyes and probably in Mahler's too, was the highest musical authority in Germany, Strauss beat a retreat. He could more easily justify a change of mind because the *Drei Pintos*, in the course of their short-lived triumphal procession across the German stage, were just then being rehearsed in Munich. On 7 April, therefore, Strauss wrote a letter of apology to Bülow.

> With the most heartfelt thanks for your kind letter, that gave me colossal

Rivalry and Friendship

pleasure, I should only like to confess how salutory has been your justified reproach concerning the *Drei Pintos*. It was dreadfully hasty of me to recommend a work for your perusal when I only knew the first act (which in conception is almost entirely by Weber and which still does not seem so bad to me, so that my lack of judgement must indeed be chronic). At the rehearsal yesterday I saw Acts II and III and completely understand your horror, they really are extremely mediocre and tedious. In the instrumentation Mahler has perpetrated some dreadful blunders, using three trumpets, trombones and tuba in the simplest passages; he constantly writes upper Fs and Gs for the oboes, and for the horns goes as high as ♪ on the F horn; and from a conductor! I now see, too, that you are quite right about the orthographic slovenliness. But the worst fifths at the end of the C major vocal trio in Act III . . . are by Weber, I saw them myself in the sketches. As I said, I knew only the first act, which Mahler had played to me on the piano with great enthusiasm; some of this must have infected me, so that I most deeply regret that you, most revered master, have been the innocent victim of my youthful rashness.[15]

Unfortunately we have no document describing Mahler's impression of Strauss and his symphony. Nor do we know how the relationship begun in Leipzig developed in the time immediately following the first meeting. We can suppose with some certainty that Mahler, who left his Leipzig post prematurely in spring 1888 and spent some time in Munich in the summer, visited Strauss on this occasion. The very first letter by Mahler to Strauss that has been preserved (p. 19) makes such a contact seem probable. Possibly, Strauss even attempted to persuade Hermann Levi to perform Mahler's First Symphony, that had been finished in March 1888, as far as a 'third conductor' could persuade a 'first' to do anything. In one of the notebooks containing Strauss's recollections we read: 'I visited him frequently in his apartment where there were fine Feuerbachs, Böcklins and Thomas on the walls, and once played [with] him the humorous funeral march from Mahler's First Symphony (about 1888), sight-reading four-handed from the manuscript score.'[16]

In October 1888 Mahler was appointed Opera Director in Budapest, an office that made such heavy demands on him that from this period of his life noticeably fewer letters by him have been preserved than from earlier or later years. The only existing letter from Mahler to Strauss from the

Rivalry and Friendship

Budapest period (p. 20) confirms, at any rate, that all contact between them had not been broken off and that personal meetings also took place.

In the autumn of 1891 we find Mahler—forced by intrigues to leave Budapest—first conductor at the Hamburg Stadttheater and Strauss—likewise forced to leave his native city Munich—second conductor in Weimar. As on many previous occasions, Hans von Bülow had helped to advance the young Strauss's career by recommending him to the Grand-Ducal Intendant at Weimar. Bülow himself, now old and in poor health, conducted the Philharmonic Concerts in Berlin and a concert cycle in Hamburg, where he lived. Bülow anecdotes were rife in the city; he and his eccentric wit were a topic of conversation in every musical circle; and as he had switched his loyalty from his previous idols Liszt and Wagner to Brahms, a native of Hamburg, he was revered as a higher being. Mahler now saw the opportunity to establish the contact with Bülow that he had striven for in vain for years, to be approved by him as a composer and perhaps even performed. He quite quickly succeeded in gaining Bülow's respect as a conductor. Testimony of this was a laurel wreath with these words on its ribbon, 'To the Pygmalion of the Hamburg Opera. Hans von Bülow.' At concerts, too, in a manner in keeping with his somewhat exalted nature, Bülow showed how much he esteemed his young colleague. While conducting he would turn towards him, pass him the score and point out particular passages to him.[17] In the autumn of 1891 Mahler had an opportunity to play him one of his compositions on the piano, and chose the first movement of his as yet unfinished C minor Symphony. While playing he looked up and saw that Bülow had his fingers to his ears.

This experience—the collapse of a hope long nurtured—was described by Mahler in a number of conversations and letters, including a letter to Richard Strauss (p. 21). This letter is written in a confiding, almost comradely tone, suggesting that the friendship between the two composers had become closer in the preceding period. Mahler must have been aware that his post at Hamburg was much more important, and also better paid, than Strauss's at Weimar. If he nevertheless presents himself as universally rejected and unrecognized—as now by Bülow—this shows us that, for him, success as a composer was the only real success. The friend in whom he confided was, however, no longer the Richard Strauss of the F minor Symphony, but a 'musician of the future'. Turning his back on the paternal influence and on strict form in general, with programmatic orchestral works like the symphonic fantasia *Aus Italien* and the symphonic poems *Macbeth*, *Don Juan* and *Tod und Verklärung*, he had conquered the concert halls as

Rivalry and Friendship

rapidly—though there was no lack of attacks by conservative critics—as he had done earlier with his wind serenade and his symphony. When, in the same letter in which he relates his rejection by Bülow, Mahler asks Strauss for the scores of *Don Juan* and *Tod und Verklärung*, this gives the impression that he may have been looking for the recipe for success that he lacked and which, in his opinion, Strauss knew. It was possibly in such a mood that Mahler crossed out the words 'Symphony in C Minor' on the cover sheet of the score he wrote in 1888, and replaced it by the title 'Totenfeier'. On 14 October 1891 he offered the symphony movement thus labelled to Schott Verlag for publication as a 'symphonic poem'.[18] From this we may infer that at that time Mahler had abandoned the idea of finishing the symphony, that is, adding further movements to it, and, in keeping with the direction taken by Strauss, was submitting a symphonic poem in a single movement. It was doubtless from such a flirtation with what he took to be the compelling fashion of the day that in 1893, when revising his First Symphony which had had its—unsuccessful—première in Budapest in 1889, he added titles borrowed from Jean Paul ('Titan', see p. 23) and E.T.A. Hoffmann ('... in the manner of Callot'), thus suggesting a programme that was of so little help to the music that he later withdrew them.

To Mahler's woeful letter of autumn 1891 Strauss seems—his reply, like almost all from that period, is lost—to have reacted in a very friendly and comradely manner. As emerges from his letter of October 1893 (p. 24) Strauss had asked his colleague two years before to send him scores, and may possibly have held out the prospect of helping to have them performed. At any rate Strauss seems in this letter, to which we unfortunately have no access, to have adopted for the first time the attitude which he then maintained towards Mahler up to the latter's death, and on which he prided himself even in his memoirs: that of the discoverer and patron whose concern it was that Mahler's costly and gigantic scores should not lie unperformed in his drawer.

Behind Mahler's hesitation between symphony and symphonic poem, and behind his toying with fanciful titles, there lay a problem that exercised Mahler himself for many years and that has worried musicology up to the present: the problem of the programmatic element in his music. Constantin Floros has attempted to demonstrate that Mahler is wrongly classified as an absolute musician and should rather be considered a typical programmatic composer.[19] His argument is based primarily on things said and written by Mahler prior to 1900, when he renounced programmes for all time. In these statements Mahler proclaims an 'inner programme' in his works and stresses that in the conception of his Second Symphony he was concerned 'never with the detailed description of a process but at most with a feeling'.[20] Taken strictly, Mahler's account of his procedure here is by no means far removed from Strauss's, who wrote the following postscript to the programme of the symphonic fantasia *Aus Italien*, written by himself: 'The frightening lack of judgement and understanding shown by the majority of critics causes them, and a large part of the public, to be induced by perhaps dazzling but purely superficial aspects of my work into misunderstanding or even completely overlooking its real content. This is made up of feelings aroused by contemplating the splendours and natural beauty of Rome and Naples, not of descriptions of them. ...'[21]

Despite this consonance, the fundamental differences of view between Mahler and Strauss should not be overlooked. These manifest themselves, for example, in their attitudes to the symphonic poems of Franz Liszt. In the summer of 1893, when Mahler added a second and third movement to *Totenfeier*—two more were to follow—he spoke to his friend Natalie Bauer-Lechner of his decision to retain the traditional designation 'symphony'.

> I have given much thought ... to what I should call my symphony, in order to give an indication of the content by the title and to comment on my intentions in one word at least. But let it always be called 'symphony' and nothing else! Terms like 'tone poem' and 'symphonic poem' are worn out without having really said anything, and one should only think of Liszt's compositions in which, without any deeper coherence, each movement depicts something of its own.[22]

Mahler's antipathy for Liszt is all the more surprising because, since his student days in Vienna, he had been a fanatical Wagnerian, and at that time partisanship of Wagner and Liszt went hand in hand. At the age of seventeen, when Strauss, still entirely under the influence of his father, condemned Wagner and was 'bored stiff' by *Siegfried*, Mahler was already a member of the Wagner Society in Vienna. All the same, he never became an adherent of Liszt and his 'New German School'.

Mahler said that his opinion of Liszt was diametrically opposed to Strauss's. 'When we last met he [Strauss] told me that he had earlier thought as little of Liszt as I do, but had later come to hold his work in highest esteem. I shall never do that. The meagre content and shoddy workmanship of his compositions are as open to view, on close inspection, as the threads of an ill-woven garment that become everywhere visible and palpable after it has been worn for a short time.'[23]

Rivalry and Friendship

Strauss had been educated in the most extreme musical conservatism by his father, the horn player Franz Strauss, revering Haydn, Mozart, Beethoven and Mendelssohn, and condemning Franz Liszt and Richard Wagner. When the 21-year-old Strauss was working under Bülow, who had long ceased being a devotee of Wagner, in Meiningen, he got to know the composer Alexander Ritter, who was a member of the Meiningen orchestra. Ritter, who, like Strauss, subsequently lived in Munich, converted the son of the anti-Wagnerian Franz Strauss to the creed of Wagner and Liszt. He explained to him the significance of these composers in the history of art, urged him to read Wagner's writings, and in so doing imparted to him all the intolerance that was as prevalent among the 'New Germans' as among their opponents. Richard Strauss's talent was too strong and original for him to become a mere imitator of Wagner or Liszt as a result of Ritter's instruction. What he took over from them as a principle of his own creation he himself formulated in his essay 'From my Youth and Apprenticeship': 'New ideas must seek new forms—this basic principle of Liszt's symphonic works, in which the poetic idea was indeed also the formative element, from then on became the guiding thread of my own symphonic works.'[24]

The clear *rapprochement* between Mahler and Strauss in 1891 suffered an interruption. At the beginning of May 1892, Strauss was taken ill with pneumonia and spent almost the whole of the following year in the Mediterranean region.

The 1893–4 season, in which Strauss resumed his service in Weimar, had brought a change in German musical life. Hans von Bülow had become so ill and frail that he could not conduct his Berlin and Hamburg concert series. Out of consideration for the invalid the organizer, Hermann Wolff, did not at first look for a successor but engaged a different conductor for almost every concert. Strauss conducted two of the Berlin concerts; in the Hamburg subscription series Strauss and Mahler took over one evening each. This development gave rise to a very intensive correspondence of which, unfortunately, again only Mahler's part is extant, as well as a personal meeting between Strauss and Mahler in January 1894. On 22 January 1894 Strauss wrote to his parents from Hamburg: 'Yesterday we had the final rehearsal, which went very well and in which (*horribile dictu*) the audience enjoyed "Mazeppa" most. I spend much time with Mahler, who is very charming and conducted a capital performance of the *Bartered Bride*, and a Dr Behn, who spoil me with their hospitality. I have been twice to Bülow's; the second time he showed himself and sat with us for an hour....'[25]

Rivalry and Friendship

Not only Mahler's personal conduct, but also his letters from this period show how hard he was trying to oblige his colleague. He invited him to stay with him the next time he visited Hamburg; he suggested Strauss might entrust the first performance of his first stage work, *Guntram*, to the Hamburg Stadttheater; he described his efforts to persuade the director, Bernhard Pollini, to accept the work; he offered Strauss 1,000 marks from his own pocket to pay the copyist. And all that before he knew the score of *Guntram*, solely on Strauss's name and on the impression Strauss had given him on the piano in Hamburg. Mahler was thus in a similar position to Strauss's earlier *vis-à-vis* the *Drei Pintos*, that he had somewhat prematurely extolled to Bülow; and Mahler corrected his attitude to *Guntram* in a similar way, probably as a result of the performance he attended in May 1894 in Weimar. To an unknown correspondent and about an unidentified work he wrote, 'Apart from *Guntram* I have never met with anything so childishly immature and at the same time so pretentious.'[26]

This verdict clearly did not apply, however, to the orchestral parts of the opera, for Mahler included the Preludes to the first and second acts of *Guntram* in his concert programmes, not only in Hamburg but in 1899 in Vienna, and even a decade later in New York.

Even after the Weimar performance Mahler tried with total commitment to have *Guntram* rehearsed at Hamburg. Director Pollini rejected the work. Perhaps his resistance was based on healthy theatrical instinct, for *Guntram* did not succeed on any German stage, but perhaps the negotiations he had had with Strauss over a post at Hamburg played a part. This is a somewhat opaque and uncongenial episode in the Mahler–Strauss relationship, uncongenial because neither of them acted with complete integrity. Mahler's first contract with the Hamburg Stadttheater was running out and Strauss, tired of the Weimar provincialism, was on the lookout for a new post. He really wanted to return—in an elevated position—to Munich, but despite many promises the negotiations became very protracted. It was in this situation that his discussions with Pollini began, though it is not known whether Strauss approached Pollini or Pollini Strauss. As early as January 1894 he wrote of his plans to his father, even mentioning the amount of his prospective annual income: 'Whether I have a lot of work and vexation here [in Weimar] or in Hamburg makes no difference; but it does make a difference whether I have a salary of 12,000M in Hamburg or 3,000 in Weimar.'[27]

Although this letter indicates that his negotiations with Pollini must have started in December 1893, he did not inform Mahler of them until the beginning of February. We know that he conducted a concert in Hamburg on 22 January and spent much time with Mahler. Despite this, he made his negotiations known in a letter—which has not been preserved—and chose, hardly by accident, the day after he had sent Mahler a piece of good news concerning the performance at his First Symphony in Weimar. Mahler showed himself very taken aback by the negotiations between Pollini and Strauss (pp. 28 and 29), but was able to announce after a few days that Pollini had offered him a new contract in which all his conditions were accepted (p. 29). This suggests that in his fear for his Hamburg post Mahler may have made a number of concessions to come to an early agreement with Pollini. That Pollini ever intended to engage Strauss and Mahler simultaneously is very unlikely, and Mahler's speculations on such a possibility (p. 29) were probably only a tactful way of concealing from Strauss that he had been worsted. Shrewd as Mahler may seem to have been in this murky affair, director Pollini was still shrewder. For it was undoubtedly, as Mahler suspected, one of Pollini's manoeuvres designed to dislodge Mahler from his 'superior present position' (p. 29). On 7 February, with the new contract just safely concluded, Mahler wrote to a Budapest colleague, the composer Ödön von Mihalovich. He was returning an opera manuscript that Mihalovich had submitted for performance at Hamburg, and wrote as if he were on the point of leaving Hamburg.

> My contract with Pollini runs out this year.... It is not as if Pollini has not tried to renew it. He was ready to make every material sacrifice; but he claims he cannot meet my artistic conditions, to which, as you know, I attach far more importance than to my personal interests; and so I am resolved once more to 'shake the dust from my feet'! As far as I know discussions are already under way with *Strauss* in Weimar, who told me he would like to be my successor here. I pity the poor fellow already, for as I know that splendid man, he too is not one for concessions.[28]

That was the first and last time that Mahler and Strauss found themselves in direct competition. They did not bear each other malice over it. In a letter to his sister Justine Mahler even admitted that he would gladly have let Strauss have his Hamburg post if there had only been a place free for him somewhere else (see p. 117). And Strauss finally got what he had wanted all along, the conducting post in Munich that he took up in the autumn of 1894.

On 12 February 1894 Hans von Bülow, the grand old man of German music, died in Cairo where he had been seeking a cure. He was the son-in-

Rivalry and Friendship

law of Franz Liszt, the first husband of his daughter Cosima; he was the prophet of Richard Wagner, a prophet whose wife Wagner took. Reacting against the experience with Wagner he became the friend and patron of Johannes Brahms; he discovered Richard Strauss and failed to recognize Gustav Mahler. Strauss had long outgrown his influence but continued to honour his mentor's memory, as we can read in his memoirs, *Erinnerungen an Hans von Bülow*: '... his touching sympathy for me, his influence in the development of my artistic capacity was—apart from the friendship of Alexander Ritter, who to the chagrin of my good father made a Wagnerian out of me—the most decisive moment in my career.'[29]

Mahler's recollections of von Bülow were of a different kind; he did not write them down. In honour of the great deceased he conducted Beethoven's 'Eroica', and the memorial service in the Hamburg Michaeliskirche gave him the inspiration for the last movement of his Second Symphony, which has provided food for thought for psychoanalysts:[30] 'You shall rise, shall rise again my flesh from brief repose....'

In the following season, 1894–5, the two young conductors so unequally treated by von Bülow became his heirs. Mahler took over the cycle of new Subscription Concerts in Hamburg, Strauss the Philharmonic Concerts in Berlin. The two crown princes, however, clearly too reckless and inexperienced, held their positions for only this one season.

As early as spring 1894 Strauss succeeded in furthering his friend Mahler's interests. He persuaded his superior, the Weimar Intendant Hans Bronsart von Schellenberg, to perform Mahler's First Symphony. For some years Bronsart had been President of the Allgemeiner Deutscher Musikverein [German Musical Society] and his word carried much weight in deciding the programme for the annual musical Festival. In 1894 this Festival—for which the somewhat archaic term *Tonkünstlerversammlung* was used—was to take place in Weimar. Strauss offered to hold the preliminary rehearsals of the First Symphony, since Mahler was not able to leave Hamburg until just before the performance.

Shortly before leaving for Weimar Mahler wrote his sister Justine, who enjoyed his complete confidence, a letter portraying his relationship to Strauss.

> ... I have spent a great deal of time with Strauss. But I should be untruthful if I said that many points of contact between us had developed.—I see more and more that I am quite alone among the musicians of today. We have divergent goals. From my standpoint I can discern

everywhere only old classical or New German pedantry. Hardly has Wagner been recognized and understood than the usual army of bigots (claiming to be the sole dispensers of salvation) come and surround the whole terrain with ramparts against true life, which always consists in changing the old, even if it is greater and more significant than the new, and in recreating it from the needs of the moment. Strauss in particular is just such a pontiff. But a likeable fellow all the same, as far as I could make him out. Whether it is all genuine has yet to be seen. All this is *between ourselves*, for he is 'of all the gods my only friend'—and I do not want to fall out with him too. Incidentally, he did speculate slightly on becoming my successor, and I should have gladly made way for him if I had only found another place.—I have tried *everything* in this direction and have nothing to reproach myself with. But it seems that my Jewishness closes all doors to me at present. . . . And I am lucky to be where I am, for as you can see from Strauss my post here is by no means the worst. . . .[31]

To understand Mahler's fundamental reserve towards the 'likeable fellow' we have to realize how intolerantly Strauss was behaving at the time and how far the 'New German pedantry' was obstructing his view of the musical scene. The New German School had come into being under Franz Liszt's leadership in close allegiance to Wagner, and had placed symphonic programme music at the centre of their creation. Their works were disseminated by the Allgemeiner Deutscher Musikverein brought into being by Liszt, and publicized by the *Neue Zeitschrift für Musik*. Through Alexander Ritter's influence Strauss became caught up in this movement. Its onesidedness did not lie in its glorification of Liszt and programme music, but in its repudiation of all other tendencies. The admissible composers included Beethoven, Weber, Berlioz, Wagner and, of course, Liszt himself. The Italians were proscribed, and likewise—leaving aside Hector Berlioz—the French, and of the Slavs at most Smetana was acknowledged. But the arch-enemy, the target of all diatribes and scorn, was Johannes Brahms. In February 1894 Mahler had seen Strauss refuse to conduct a concert because he had been asked, in memory of Bülow, to include a work by Brahms.

Mahler, although a Wagnerian, was not a doctrinaire musician. He advocated Piotr Ilyich Tchaikovsky and Bedřich Smetana; he was among the admirers of Mascagni; he espoused the cause of a—now forgotten—opera, *Joseph and his Brothers*, by Étienne Méhul, and did not even draw back before Giacomo Meyerbeer. The work he happened to be rehearsing

Rivalry and Friendship

was accorded his complete devotion. Mahler undoubtedly also rehearsed Brahms's Third Symphony with enthusiasm for the Hamburg concert, for he held Brahms in high esteem despite having been, since his student days, a disciple of Anton Bruckner. Throughout his life Mahler kept aloof from all factions and sided only with quality. Even his antipathy for Liszt did not prevent him from appreciating and arranging performances of his *Legende von der heiligen Elisabeth*.

At the thirtieth Festival of the Allgemeiner Deutscher Musikverein in Weimar the operas *Guntram* by Richard Strauss and *Hansel and Gretel* by Engelbert Humperdinck were presented. The main symphonic work of the Festival was Mahler's First Symphony, which at the time bore the title 'Titan'. The work had an unfavourable reception, on account of inadequate preparation, the confusing title Mahler had devised while revising the score and undoubtedly also because of the formal difficulties the work posed to the audience of the time. Until the end of Mahler's life it remained the child of sorrow among his symphonic offspring. A Hamburg friend collected the mostly negative reviews and sent them to Mahler at the Attersee where he was spending his vacation. In mid-June Mahler acknowledged receiving them: 'Many thanks for sending the reviews. I found them most diverting. You do not know the drollest of them, which came to me from another quarter. . . . *Str.* is *not* entirely above suspicion! His favourite critic is the author of the *worst* reviews!'[32]

What had taken place between Strauss and Mahler in Weimar, and what caused Mahler to harbour and express this monstrous suspicion of Strauss—for only he can have been meant—is not known. Nor can it be ascertained exactly who is meant by the favourite critic. The epithet would best fit Arthur Seidl, a friend of Strauss's youth, or the Berlin music editor Otto Lessmann. Possibly Strauss made a critical comment during the rehearsals or after the performance of 'Titan', to which Mahler reacted sensitively. Even in his mature years—as we shall see—he could not endure criticism from Strauss, although he cared little for the opinion of others. The objections Strauss raised to the Symphony are known to us because he communicated them to Mahler in writing. Although Strauss's letter is lost, we can infer from Mahler's reply that Strauss had advised him to shorten the final movement, which Mahler declined to do, giving detailed reasons (p. 37).

We should not, however, conclude from this suggestion that Strauss saw no merit in the First Symphony. The critic Ernst Otto Nodnagel, who heard the work on 3 June 1894 in Weimar and misunderstood it entirely, wrote later that Strauss had been among the few people who found 'the music new, but not confused'.[33] One might even say that apart from his favourite, the Fourth Symphony, Strauss valued the First Symphony most of all among Mahler's works.

The failure of the First Symphony in Weimar did not deter Strauss from including a further work by Mahler in the programme of the Berlin concert series he was conducting as Bülow's successor, the three instrumental movements of the Second Symphony. As Strauss was a newcomer to Berlin and Mahler was as good as unknown, this represented a risk, though Strauss was clearly encouraged by the concert organizer Hermann Wolff. In the programme of his forty-ninth Philharmonic Concert on 4 March 1895 Strauss included the first three movements of the unpublished symphony, and invited Mahler to conduct the performance himself. Also present at this concert was the Austrian composer Wilhelm Kienzl, who sat between Strauss and the conductor Carl Muck in a box.

> The theme of the first movement, vigorously introduced by the double basses and developed expansively, impressed me. In the further course of the movement that held my attention throughout, all kinds of harmonic and instrumental audacities were to be heard, particularly a stubbornly dissonant fortissimo passage for the brass. Richard Strauss, who was taking a rest from conducting during this number, had invited Muck and myself to sit with him in an empty box to enjoy Mahler's work together. At the passage for brass just mentioned Strauss, sitting on my left, turns to me with enthusiasm in his eyes, 'Believe me, there are no limits to musical expression!' At the same time, to my right, Muck's face is distorted with unmistakable revulsion and the single word, 'Horrible!' comes from between his teeth. I, 'the worldling betwixt', was moved to reflect on the divergent effects of art on natures differently constituted and on the eminent subjectivity of all artistic enjoyment.[34]

The response to Mahler's C minor Symphony was negative, and decades later Strauss recalled that Otto Lessmann, the publisher of the *Allgemeine Musikzeitung*, had scolded him with the words, 'the altar that Bülow consecrated has now been fouled by pygmies'.[35]

Lessmann, who was active in the Allgemeiner Deutscher Musikverein, and like-minded people, no doubt took care that for seven years Mahler's name did not appear on their Festival programmes. Strauss, by contrast, was an unwavering admirer of the Second Symphony and recommended his father to hear it when Mahler conducted the work at a concert of the

Rivalry and Friendship

Hugo Wolf Society in the autumn of 1900: 'On 20 October Mahler is conducting his C minor Symphony in Munich, a very interesting work. If you want to hear the general rehearsal, you need only write a few lines to Arthur Seidl (the secretary of the Hugo Wolf Society).'[36]

In 1895 and 1896, when their correspondence became sparser again after the prolific *Guntram* and *Titan* period, both composers worked for the first and last time in their lives on the same artistic task, the setting to music of Friedrich Nietzsche. How different were their temperaments and approaches, and how divergent their interpretations of Nietzsche, can be heard from the two works that sprang from this interaction of philosophy and music. Strauss, in keeping with his tendency, produced a symphonic poem in one movement lasting a good half-hour, entitled *Also sprach Zarathustra*. It is his most serious, most reserved work, the one most closely related to absolute music, from that period. Mahler composed a symphony in six movements lasting one-and-a-half hours that was originally furnished with movement titles and subtitles and was to be called 'Meine fröhliche Wissenschaft'. By the time it went to print, however, Mahler was a declared opponent of all programmes and unceremoniously discarded the carefully considered and often-changed titles. All that remained of Nietzsche was the poem 'O man, take heed!' from Zarathustra which, entrusted to an alto voice, forms the fourth movement of the symphony.

While Strauss translated his thoughts and feelings on reading Nietzsche's *Zarathustra* into music, Mahler's Third Symphony, leaving aside the alto solo, has little to do with Nietzsche. He wanted to give musical expression to the whole of Nature—from inanimate rock through flowers and animals to man, and beyond that to the divine. The pagan Pan or Dionysus of the first movement might still be thought of as Nietzschean. But in the last movement the divine is embodied in Christian love of one's neighbour and the motto, 'Father contemplate my wounds! Let no being be forsaken!'

The musicologist Ludwig Schiedermair, who knew both composers in his youth and described them as antipodes, pointed explicitly to what they had in common, the concern with Nietzsche.

> Like Richard Strauss, Gustav Mahler was affected by Nietzsche's spirituality. It is not that either tried to dissolve and convert Nietzsche's ideas directly into music, but rather that they were inspired by them to produce basic ideas of their own work. More extensively than Strauss in his *Zarathustra* (of 1896) Mahler grappled over and again with

Rivalry and Friendship

Nietzsche's thought—as his spoken and written statements to me also testify—driven by an unrelenting urge to escape the discord in his own nature. However much they differed in their physical and intellectual make-up, they yet agreed in their adherence to Nietzsche's art, and in their productive reaction to the challenge of programme music....[37]

Mahler would not have been pleased to hear this in his later years, as he repudiated not only programme music but Nietzsche as well. When, on a journey in 1906, he was asked by the composer Bernard Scharlitt about his 'point of contact' with Strauss, the musical arrangement of Nietzsche, he sidestepped the real problem: 'The explanation is simply that we both, as musicians, sensed what I might call the latent music in Nietzsche's mighty work....'[38]

Strauss completed his 'Symphonic poem after Nietzsche' in August 1896, and Mahler the first movement of his Third Symphony, the only one of the six that was still missing, at about the same time. In the same year, at the end of November 1896, Strauss conducted the first performance of *Zarathustra* at a concert of the Frankfurt Museumsgesellschaft. Mahler had to wait until 1902 for a complete performance of his symphony, and would perhaps have waited longer had not Strauss come to his aid. Who, in face of such inequality before the public, could have entirely suppressed envy or jealousy? Mahler could not. The Czech composer Josef Bohuslav Foerster, who was a close friend of Mahler's in his Hamburg period, observed how preoccupied Mahler was with the 'Strauss case': 'Right at the beginning of our friendship I noticed that Mahler saw in Strauss his only rival; he got hold of each of his scores, that were appearing in quick succession at J. Aibl's in Munich at the time, immersed himself in them, talked about them and made a number of pertinent criticisms, which were always well-founded and without a trace of denigration.'[39]

By the expression 'his only rival' Foerster probably meant that Mahler saw in Strauss his only equal, the only one who counted for him. But perhaps he also used it because he remembered that at that time, in the 'nineties, Mahler had not been free of jealousy. Just as he had once, in Leipzig, envied Arthur Nikisch his fame as a conductor, he now witnessed the young Strauss's success with the critics with a vexation to which he sometimes gave utterance: 'Take the Strauss case! They [the critics] now proclaim with mighty complacency that the days of unrecognized genius are over. For behold: hardly has he appeared than we trumpet his praises! Hurrah: from now on geniuses will be paid forthwith in cash!'[40]

Rivalry and Friendship

To the symphonic poems by Strauss already mentioned, the highly effective *Till Eulenspiegel* had recently been added. Mahler studied the new scores not only to learn from them, but also, no doubt, to mark himself off from them, to preserve his own sound and his own form. He drew the distinction above all by revising his attitude to programme music. Not at one stroke, not from one day to the next, but as part of a protracted process. He started in 1896 with the suppression of the title 'Titan' and all the subtitles of the First Symphony, and ended in 1900 with a radical renunciation of programmes and all literary auxiliaries.

Mahler, it is true, had never composed programme music as practised by Strauss, had never tried out the sculptural gestures of the *Eulenspiegel* music. The autobiographical element in his works had nothing in common with Strauss's self-portrayal in the *Heldenleben*. That the problems of programme music were, for Mahler, connected with his relationship to Strauss, however, is revealed by his brief correspondence with the music journalist Arthur Seidl, a friend of Strauss's youth. Of this correspondence too only Mahler's contribution has been preserved, but the content of Seidl's letter can be inferred, since Mahler quotes from it in his reply of 17 February 1897.

> It is curious how you have given me in a sense a clarification of myself. You have very aptly characterized my goals in contrast to those of Strauss. You are right that my 'music attains to a programme as its final intellectual elucidation, whereas in Strauss the programme is given from the outset as a task to be performed'.—I believe that in this you have touched on the great enigmas of our time, and at the same time stated the either/or confronting us.

Mahler goes on in his letter to Arthur Seidl to set out the principles of his composition, and finally expresses his gratification that recently a few of his works have been performed.

> I shall never forget that the initial impulse to produce them was given to me by Strauss in a truly magnanimous way. But no one should think I see myself as his 'competitor' (as unfortunately often happens).—I repeat that I cannot regard two such people as a 'subtraction sum'. Leaving aside the fact that I should doubtless appear with my works as a monstrosity had not Strauss's successes paved the way for me, I see it as my greatest pleasure to have found such a comrade-in-arms and fellow creator among my contemporaries. Schopenhauer somewhere uses the

Rivalry and Friendship

image of two miners tunnelling from opposite directions, who meet on their subterranean paths. This seems aptly to sum up my relationship to Strauss.—How lonely I should feel and how hopeless would my striving seem if I could not see such 'signs and miracles' as auguring future triumph. When in a way so flattering to me you refer to us both as the 'opposed poles' of the new magnetic axis, you express a view that I have long harboured in secret....[41]

In the autumn of 1897 Mahler attained the highest position open to an opera conductor at that time: by a decree of 8 October the Emperor Franz Joseph I appointed him director of his Imperial and Royal Opera in Vienna. Six months previously Strauss had announced to his parents that 'G. Mahler is replacing Jahn at Vienna'.[42] Strauss was still in Munich, this being his fourth year there, but though he was Court Conductor with the same power as Hermann Levi had had, he had only a two-year contract. As a composer and conductor of his own works Strauss had by now succeeded in carrying his fame far beyond Germany's borders. At the time when Mahler was granted his Imperial appointment, Strauss was conducting two concerts at the Amsterdam Concertgebouw, in which, with works by Beethoven, Wagner and Berlioz, he presented two of his own symphonic poems. In mid-November we find him in Barcelona with a programme that included three of his own compositions, and a few days later, on 21 November, in Brussels, where, at a popular concert, he played only his own works. Immediately afterwards he went to Paris and London, where Strauss songs and the symphonic poems *Till Eulenspiegel* and *Tod und Verklärung* were performed.

The situation, therefore, was the same as it had been ten years previously. Mahler still had an advantage as opera conductor, and Strauss as composer. To begin with the Court Opera made such demands on Mahler that he had no time for anything else. In his first Vienna season (1897–8) he conducted more than a hundred performances, in addition to rehearsals, negotiations and administration. 'Please don't take it amiss that I don't write more,' he says in one letter to Strauss of the time. 'I am up to my eyes in work.' (See p. 46.)

In the autumn of 1898 Strauss left Munich and, with a ten-year contract in his pocket, went as 'Royal Prussian Conductor' to the Berlin Opera. Strauss was thus in the German capital and would have been at the goal of his desires had he been at once entrusted with a concert series. Mahler in Vienna was more fortunate in this respect, for in the autumn of 1898 he took

Rivalry and Friendship

over as conductor of the Philharmonic Concerts in addition to his opera duties. In his first season, on 19 February 1899, a composers' concert took place in which Siegfried Wagner, Wilhelm Kienzl and Engelbert Humperdinck conducted their own works. At this concert Mahler conducted the Preludes to the first and second acts of *Guntram*. Undoubtedly, the original intention was for Strauss himself to interpret one of his works. We must therefore assume that Strauss was not available and asked his old friend Mahler to conduct in his place. The absence of any correspondence relating to this concert shows that not only letters by Strauss but a number of Mahler's have been lost over the years.

In November 1899 Mahler performed the symphonic fantasia *Aus Italien* at a Philharmonic concert. There is no trace of this performance in the extant correspondence, indicating another gap.

It is not until 1900 that we can again observe the usual communications between Strauss and Mahler. On 9 April 1900 Strauss performed three orchestral songs by Mahler at a concert of the Wagner Society in Berlin. Shortly afterwards he offered Mahler a ballet for performance at the Vienna Opera, which Mahler accepted without seeing it, but which Strauss never composed (see p. 47 and p. 48). Strauss's letter contains a number of postscripts, including a warning against the Vienna Gesellschaft der Autoren, Komponisten und Musikverleger (an association of authors, composers and music publishers), the head of which was Mahler's publisher Josef Weinberger. Strauss was involved at the time in setting up a society in which only composers and not publishers were represented.

In January 1901 Strauss appeared at the head of the Kaim Orchestra in Vienna with a programme of his own works including the symphonic poem *Ein Heldenleben*. During this visit a personal meeting between Strauss and Mahler took place, probably the first for a considerable period. Their conversations inaugurated a period of close contact and abundant correspondence, from which, fortunately, a number of letters by Strauss have been preserved. During his visit to Vienna Strauss seems to have spoken of his new opera *Feuersnot*; he probably also played from it, as was his custom, for at the outset of the correspondence we are in the midst of deliberations concerning the Vienna performance.

At the beginning of June Strauss went to the thirty-seventh Festival of the Allgemeiner Deutscher Musikverein, which took place that year at Heidelberg. His intention, as he wrote to his parents, was to conduct some of his own works, 'and to unseat Herr von Hase in the General Assembly; perhaps the rest of the committee will fall with him: Steinbach, Lessmann, etc. It will be a jolly fight....'[43] Strauss emerged victorious from this affray: he was elected First President of the Musikverein, and of the old governing committee only Otto Lessmann survived. The defeated Herr von Hase was head of a publishing house (Breitkopf & Härtel), and so belonged to a group with which Strauss was in violent conflict at that time. With the election of Strauss as President a new era began in the life of the venerable society, which was of great importance for the development and propagation of new music. Richard Strauss, in his Weimar period still a one-sided 'pontiff' given to 'New German pedantry', had undergone a process of artistic and human maturing that impelled him to keep the Musikverein's Festivals open to all musical tendencies. Naturally, Strauss did not himself make the selection from the 250 or so compositions that were submitted each year. The work was shared by a number of committee members, but Strauss set the guidelines for selection: 'He stressed in the most unmistakable way our common duty, *sine ira et studio*, to let anyone have his say who had any right to do so—however much our personal feelings might incline us otherwise. We should be on our guard against all cliquish preferences and invite not even a suspicion of one-sidedness.'[44]

Even a witness as impartial as Bruno Walter recalls the Allgemeiner Deutscher Musikverein in the friendliest terms: '... I should like to observe in retrospect that the selection of contemporary works of the most divergent tendencies and styles gave a thoroughly favourable impression of the committee's open-mindedness. I can, indeed, think of the services of the Allgemeiner Deutscher Musikverein to musical life in Germany, its fresh and progressive spirit and its serious sense of responsibility, only with great respect.'[45]

However, we know of at least one case in which Strauss by-passed his committee to accept a work for the forthcoming Festival: the Third Symphony by Gustav Mahler (p. 52) which, although completed in 1896, had not until then been performed in its entirety. In the following years, at the Society's Festivals, Mahler's Second Symphony (in Basle), the *Kindertotenlieder* and other songs (in Graz) and the Sixth Symphony (in Essen) were performed.

In the same year as he was elected President of the Allgemeiner Deutscher Musikverein, 1901, Strauss took over as conductor of a concert series in Berlin. Although he had now been established in Berlin for almost three years, up to now he had only occasionally had an opportunity to conduct concerts. The Philharmonic Concerts were conducted by Arthur Nikisch, the concerts of the Royal Orchestra by Felix Weingartner, both of

Rivalry and Friendship

whom were honoured by the critics and worshipped by the public. Strauss finally discovered a gap that he could fill. As modern music was neglected in the established concert series, he put on concerts of new works, starting with six in the 1901–2 season. For these he was not able to use the Royal Orchestra, but the Berlin Tonkünstlerorchester, increased to ninety players. If we consider his position in the Allgemeiner Deutscher Musikverein together with these concerts, we realize that no other artist of the time had as much influence on modern music as Strauss. That he used his power wisely is attested not only by many artists but not least by the concert programmes in which he helped Anton Bruckner to achieve the recognition he deserved and presented such diverse personalities as Hans Pfitzner, Piotr Ilyich Tchaikovsky, Ignacy Paderewski, Edward Elgar and Gustave Charpentier. At one of Strauss's first concerts of new works Mahler conducted his Fourth Symphony—a few weeks after its Munich first performance. In a letter to another Berlin concert organizer Strauss explains why he attached so much importance to Mahler's Fourth.

> You know that I can only perform new works. I have already come to grief with Bruckner's D minor. But this had been rehearsed too much to be dropped. Mahler's Fourth is my main attraction; the Third is not performable here for the time being because of its large orchestra and chorus. The First and Second Mahler has already conducted here himself. Now your concerts are not so exclusively devoted to new works as mine. Why don't you let Mahler conduct his First or Second Symphony on 2 December? It can do the Berlin public no harm to hear these difficult works quite often. But unfortunately I cannot give up the Fourth, I owe this to the whole company which, as you know, is not my personal affair.
>
> Please do the Second Symphony and the splendid *Klagende Lied* (that is a new work). Chorus and soloists are always at your disposal....[46]

Although Strauss originally intended to conduct himself, pressed by Mahler he ceded the rostrum to the composer. Mahler's old friend Natalie Bauer-Lechner reported with satisfaction on the symphony's reception by the audience and above all by Strauss himself.

> Richard Strauss, whom the work interested more from one rehearsal to the next, was finally quite carried away by it, particularly the third movement, saying that he could not write such an adagio. He also told Mahler afterwards, with a large number of people present, that he had

Rivalry and Friendship

learned an extraordinary amount from him. 'I have had an especially good look at your Second Symphony, and assimilated much from it.' As a sign of his esteem Strauss afterwards sent him the scores of his entire works.[47]

During this stay in Berlin, Mahler and Strauss had a conversation concerning artistic fundamentals, of which we unfortunately know only the little that Mahler related in a letter to his fiancée, Alma Schindler. These lines, taken out of the context of the whole letter, are very frequently quoted. Mahler's statement that he had 'talked very seriously with Strauss in Berlin and tried to show him the cul-de-sac he was in', cannot be understood as it stands. But if Mahler's letter to Alma is read in its entirety, we can see the chain of ideas that led him to mention the Berlin discussion with Strauss at this point, and the context also reveals the content of this discussion. It revolved around the programme in music.

As early as 1896 Mahler had, as we have seen (p. 122), begun to distance himself from the literary programme when he withdrew the titles of his First Symphony. The Third Symphony, too, copiously subtitled in the manuscript, went to press without these programmatic indications. In the autumn of 1900 Mahler's antipathy to the programme reached its highest point so far. He was in Munich to conduct a performance of his Second Symphony. After the concert he retired with friends and admirers to the Park Hotel to bring the evening to a convivial end. The conversation came round to programmes and programme notes.

> It was as if lightning had struck a calm sunny landscape. Mahler's eyes shone more than ever, his brow furrowed, he rose excitedly from the table and proclaimed in an emotional voice, 'Away with programmes that arouse false notions. Leave the audience its own thoughts on the work being performed; do not force it to read while the music is being played; do not teach it to be prejudiced! If a composer has imparted to his listeners the feelings that flowed through him, his goal is attained. The language of sound has come close to words, but has revealed infinitely more than they can express. . . .'[48]

A year had passed since this Munich declaration, which soon went the rounds in music circles. After Mahler had conducted his Fourth Symphony for Strauss in Berlin he travelled to Dresden to attend rehearsals of his Second. At the wish of the King of Saxony he composed a guide to the work, a programme that, while not explicating individual musical themes or passages, nevertheless put into words the emotional content of individual movements and the metaphysical questions they raised. Mahler discusses this programme for the Second Symphony in his letter to Alma before coming by simple association to Strauss.

> The Second goes off here today. My Almschi! Justi has not told you that this programme was written for a superficial, helpless person (you know whom) and only gives externalities—the mere surface of the matter—as finally does every programme of a musical work. And this for a work which is so unified and self-contained, that it can no more be explained than the world.—For I am convinced that if God were asked to give his programme for the 'world' he has created, he would be equally unable to do so.—At most we should then have a 'revelation' that reveals as much of the nature of God and life as my programme does to my C minor. Indeed, it would lead directly—like all religions of revelation—to misunderstanding, incomprehension, to a simplification and coarsening and finally a distortion that makes the work and above all its creator unrecognizable.—I have just talked very seriously with Strauss in Berlin and tried to show him the cul-de-sac he is in. But unfortunately he could not entirely follow me. He is a very likeable fellow and his relationship to me is touching. And yet I can be nothing to him—since I can see all of him but he only my pedestal.—He is shortly coming to Vienna. Perhaps I shall bring him out to see you.—[49]

This passage makes clear that Mahler mistakenly believed his colleague to be caught in the 'cul-de-sac' of descriptive symphonic poems, rather than on his *via triumphalis* to the opera stage. And yet it was precisely Mahler who could have foreseen this development, for he had declared as early as 1896 that music was standing 'at the great crossroads where the two divergent paths of symphonic and dramatic music ... part for ever'.[50] If this idea ever found confirmation, it was in Mahler's own progression to the great instrumental symphonies and in the simultaneous metamorphosis of Strauss into musical dramatist.

In December 1901, however, nothing was yet decided. The Berlin conversation might have led to a deeper relationship between the two artists. But it turned out differently. Their subsequent meetings took place under different auspices, for Mahler had become engaged shortly before leaving on his trip to Germany and announced the engagement to his unsuspecting friends at the turn of the year. Strauss was among those congratulating him (p. 65). Mahler's circle of friends in Vienna was made up of people of his age with whom he had shared his joys and sorrows for more than twenty years, a kind of self-appointed family whose spiritual head, strangely, was not Mahler but the poet Siegfried Lipiner. Within a few days Alma succeeded in estranging her fiancé from these friends, who appeared to her too old and insignificant. It may be that Mahler's friends, especially Lipiner and Natalie Bauer-Lechner, also made mistakes, that they did not receive his young fiancée with sufficient cordiality, and underestimated her spirit, particularly her fighting spirit. It will surprise no one that Alma emerged victorious and his old companions vanished from Gustav Mahler's life. This happened in mid-January 1902. A few days later Richard Strauss and his wife Pauline came to Vienna to see the première of *Feuersnot* and to give two concerts. The day before the performance Strauss wrote to his parents: 'Yesterday, Monday, final rehearsal of *Feuersnot* under Mahler which unfortunately, because of his dreadful nervousness, did not go so well as the Saturday rehearsal had led us to expect, when, above all, the glorious Vienna orchestra delighted me utterly. It is decidedly the best orchestra in Europe, with the most beautiful sound.'[51]

Strauss had been married since 1894 to the opera and concert singer Pauline de Ahna, who had once been his pupil and who had sung the main female part in the Weimar performance of *Guntram*. Pauline Strauss-de Ahna was known not only as a masterly interpreter of her husband's songs, but as a woman of unpredictable temperament and total lack of constraint. In the relationship between Strauss and Mahler up to now she had played virtually no part, but the moment Mahler was engaged, and soon afterwards married, it was a matter of course that the two wives became involved in it.

Alma gave a detailed description of her first meeting with Richard and Pauline Strauss in her book on Mahler. She also wrote in this connection that Mahler had not conducted the first performance 'because he had an aversion to the work'.[52] She was wrong! For Mahler, as the records of the Court Opera show, had not only rehearsed *Feuersnot* but had conducted the première, and only handed the work over after the third performance when he left on his honeymoon. If such an error is possible, we must treat the account of the other events of this première evening with caution, although Alma generally bases herself on her diary.

At the end of January there was the première of *Feuersnot* by Richard Strauss. Pauline Strauss watched the performance with us in our box. She raged the whole time: no one could like this botched piece of work, we were dishonestly pretending to like it but knew as well as she that there was not an original note in it, everything was stolen, from Wagner, from many others, even from Schillings ('Maxi' as she called him) whom she far preferred to her husband. In short, she was raving....[53]

In 1946, in the library of his friend and biographer Willi Schuh in Zürich, Richard Strauss discovered Alma's book, read it and annotated it in the margin. He lacked the documents in Switzerland to correct Alma's error regarding the conductor of the Vienna first performance. But to the passage just quoted describing Frau Strauss in the opera box, he added the following marginal note that reflects his bafflement: 'Totally unbelievable! At any rate entirely fabricated, or at least it is a mystery on which misunderstanding this whole story is based. The more so as my wife always particularly liked *Feuersnot*.'[54]

The scene in the opera box is followed in Alma's account by a violent quarrel between the Strausses, ending with Frau Pauline returning to her hotel and refusing to take part in the première dinner.

We went on ahead to our table without speaking a word. Strauss soon came, visibly exhausted, sat down beside me and said, in these exact words, 'My wife is often dreadfully rude, but, you know, it is something I need.' Strauss showed himself to me in his true colours that evening. During the meal he had no other thought than 'money'. He constantly pestered Mahler to calculate the royalties to be anticipated from a large or a moderate success, sat the whole evening with a pencil in his hand, put it behind his ear from time to time in a semi-jocular way, in short he behaved like a commercial traveller.[55]

Perhaps Mahler, still preoccupied with the première that had awakened his 'productive powers' too, would have paid no attention to Strauss's calculations of royalties. He had known Strauss for fifteen years, was aware of his intellectual interests and also of his business sense. But Alma called back the memory of the première evening in a letter she sent after him to the Semmering where he had taken a few days' refuge. Alma's letter, like most of the letters sent to Mahler, has been lost. We can only guess at its contents from Mahler's reaction.

At breakfast I received your dear letter, which gives me inexpressible joy.... Not only the parting, the whole evening was unsatisfying to me. The atmosphere Strauss spreads around him is so sobering—one becomes thoroughly estranged from oneself. If these are the fruits that hang from a tree, how can one love the tree? Your observation on him hit

Rivalry and Friendship

the mark. And I am proud that you hit on the truth so spontaneously. Is it not so: rather eat the bread of poverty together and walk in the light, than lose oneself like that to triviality. The time will come when people will see the wheat winnowed from the chaff—and my time will come when his is over....

Your remark the evening before last, 'You take no part in the conversation', you will now be able to answer yourself.—What could I reply to these coffee house phrases at such an exalted moment, after such a performance, which awakens my own productive powers too, and that ought to free us from everyday things, not lead us into the midst of squalor, like a conversation about royalties and capital (the constant dreams of St.'s fantasy, almost indivisible from his enthusiasms).[56]

This letter is not easy to interpret. What a difference from Mahler's attitude six weeks before when he had wanted to help the 'dear fellow' out of his 'cul-de-sac'! Perhaps Mahler needed to show himself in his true light before his future bride, who had taken exception to Strauss's preoccupation with business. Perhaps he liked to feel himself cast in a role of moral superiority because he felt inferior in matters of money-making. Perhaps the jealousy subliminally present in the Hamburg days had caught him out.

Mahler was by no means the unworldly dreamer and ascetic that his disciples later made of him. Although generous with it, he knew the value of money. He also knew how to look after his business interests, and was in no danger of having to eat 'the bread of poverty'. Nevertheless, the commercial aspects of his profession were uncongenial to him because they distracted him from the real thing—art. His annoyance at Strauss's behaviour on the première evening is therefore understandable; what is surprising is the solemn tone and the biblical diction, which at this stage of his life flowed to Mahler's pen only at moments of great inner agitation. We can therefore assume that Mahler was not only annoyed, but moved at deeper levels. Such solemnity could only announce a personal injury or a painful disappointment. Mahler uses the image of 'the wheat and the chaff' again in connection with Strauss several years later, in a letter of January 1907. After a performance of *Salome* conducted by Strauss in Berlin, Mahler wrote to his wife: 'Deeply at work in it, under a mass of rubble, is a live volcano, a subterranean fire—not a mere firework! It is probably the same with Strauss's whole personality! That is what makes it so hard to separate the wheat from the chaff in him. But I have enormous respect for the phenomenon as a whole, and have now reaffirmed it. I am immensely glad!'[57]

Rivalry and Friendship

Mahler's contradictory judgement on his colleague can only be explained by contradictions in himself. In 1907 he was glad that Strauss would not be counted as chaff before history, but that wheat and chaff, rubble and volcanic powers, lay one over the other in him and that he, Mahler, could love and respect him, which was for him clearly a genuine need.

The first meeting after the Vienna première of *Feuersnot* must have been in June 1902 at the Festival of the Allgemeiner Deutscher Musikverein in Krefeld. Strauss had put Mahler's Third Symphony on the programme, the first movement of which was still unperformed, and which was now to be heard as a whole for the first time. Alma Mahler reports as follows on this first performance.

> After the first movement there was an outburst of jubilation. Richard Strauss went right to the front of the podium and applauded so ostentatiously that he really sealed the success of the movement. And after every movement the audience seemed more enthralled ... Strauss became more and more passive, and finally invisible....
>
> Later the same evening Strauss showed himself in all his coldness. We had dined in a small restaurant. In going past, Strauss patronizingly gave each of us his hand and walked on without noticing Mahler's terrible excitement, without saying a single word to him. Mahler felt this deeply and remained for a while silent and downcast. The whole outward success now seemed worthless to him.[58]

In 1903 the relationship between Strauss and Mahler was enriched by a new aspect. Since the turn of the century Strauss and a friend from his youth, Friedrich Rösch, had been fighting for a reform of the copyright law that would secure more rights and larger incomes for composers. At the same time a performing rights society was brought into being, the Genossenschaft deutscher Tonsetzer, that was incorporated in 1903. Three years earlier Strauss had expressly warned Mahler in a letter (p. 47) against the Vienna Gesellschaft der Autoren, Komponisten und Musikverleger (AKM) of which Mahler had been a member since 1897. Strauss and his Genossenschaft were opposed from the start to the AKM because it included music publishers who, in Strauss's opinion, set the tone. At the beginning of 1903 Strauss seems to have begun, in a letter that has not been preserved, to woo Mahler away from the Vienna AKM. Mahler (p. 72) showed distinct interest, but wanted to make his final decision only after a personal meeting with Strauss. This conversation is likely to have taken

Rivalry and Friendship

place in March 1903, when Strauss conducted a concert of the Berlin Tonkünstlerorchester in Vienna.

What passed between them we unfortunately do not know. Alma Mahler, usually an assiduous observer of all things relating to Strauss, has not a word to say on these discussions and their outcome. Perhaps future research will bring new material to light. We know today only that Strauss succeeded in securing Mahler's defection from the Vienna association, since he resigned at the end of 1903. In October 1903 Mahler corresponded on this matter with Friedrich Rösch[59] and consulted his lawyer. Nothing is known about his admission to the Genossenschaft deutscher Tonsetzer. That he joined is proved by a letter written to Mahler by the Vienna publisher Josef Stritzko. This very revealing letter, reproduced below, must, however, be approached with some caution since Stritzko, Mahler's Vienna publisher, was naturally involved in the conflict of interests with the Genossenschaft.

Vienna
5 May 1904

Herr Director Gustav Mahler,

I have made careful enquiries concerning the Genossenschaft deutscher Tonsetzer but with great regret I must inform you that, as a result of signatures given by yourself, it is impossible for me to act successfully in both your interests and our own. You approached us previously with a request to release you with respect to the Vienna Autorengesellschaft, and we met your request in order to oblige you.

We were, however, of the opinion that you, Herr Director, or your representative, would come to such an agreement with the Genossenschaft as would promote the dissemination of your work rather than hindering it. But you have not only submitted yourself to the statutes of this society; you have also agreed to recognize the performance fees demanded by the Genossenschaft, and indeed, the rights to all your registered compositions that have appeared under our imprint are retained by that society even if you should cease to be a member. In this the Genossenschaft does not protect your and our interests, but uses you to force concert organizers to reach agreements with them. In this way major performances of your symphonic works have already been prevented, from which we must both suffer considerably. Further performances are now envisaged, but I fear that these too will not come about for the same reason. At all events I beg you, Herr Director, to come to an understanding with the Genossenschaft through your representative Dr Emil Freund; for if it continues to impose performance fees of 250–400M, the propagation of your work is virtually ruled out. I have looked at our contract, hoping to find a point that might entitle us to intervene as publishers, but unfortunately the only point that would have given us this right has been annulled by the permission granted you to resign from the Vienna Gesellschaft in order to join the Genossenschaft. Try to have your works freed by the intervention of your German friends, Richard Strauss, etc., or at least to have the performance fees reduced to not more than 50–100M. You are the more likely to achieve this as it seems to me impossible that such large contributions are demanded for works by Richard Strauss or others. On this point your representative Dr E. Freund could no doubt ask for clarification.

Yours very respectfully
Stritzko[60]

What happened subsequently, what steps Mahler took or omitted to take, has not yet been discovered. The correspondence between Mahler and Strauss is of no help here, nor are Mahler's hitherto published letters to his lawyer, Emil Freund. All that is certain is that he did not rejoin the Vienna Gesellschaft. The high fees demanded by the German league do not appear to have damaged the dissemination of Mahler's works, for it was precisely in 1903 and 1904 that Mahler, the previously unperformed composer, made the breakthrough he longed for. His symphonies I to IV, and after the autumn of 1904, the Fifth as well, were performed in many German cities with himself or others conducting; and in the Netherlands, where Strauss had scored successes as early as 1897, Mahler's work found a musical home from 1903 on. In October 1903 he wrote to his wife from Amsterdam: 'After the final chord a quite imposing burst of applause. Everyone tells me there has been nothing like it in living memory. Strauss, who is much in vogue here, has been beaten handsomely.'[61]

When Strauss read this in 1946 he put a question mark and an exclamation mark in the margin.

In 1905 Strauss and Mahler were linked in more mutual undertakings than in all previous or subsequent years. At the end of May the first Alsatian Musical Festival took place in Strasbourg, with the aim of opposing German music to French in peaceful rivalry. The concert programmes, however, reflected this elevated objective of cultural politics rather imperfectly, as French music was represented only by César Franck and Gustave

Rivalry and Friendship

Charpentier, who had to contend with Beethoven, Brahms, Mozart, Wagner, Strauss and Mahler. Strauss conducted a Mozart concert and his *Symphonia domestica*, Mahler performed his Fifth Symphony and a whole Beethoven evening with the Ninth as it culmination. According to Alma Mahler's report, Mahler had numerous rehearsals and 'glorious' performances. Strauss, on the other hand, who allegedly attended only the final rehearsal: 'was filled with alarm at the prospect of his performance. He foamed at the mouth, became violent in his rage. The *Domestica*: a dreadful performance, not one entry was right.'[62]

The impression made on the audience seems to have been different. The French writer Romain Rolland, who esteemed Mahler highly and saw in Strauss the 'first musical personality of Europe', while criticizing the way in which Mozart, under Strauss, had 'taken on a stormy, violent aspect',[63] called Mahler's interpretation of Beethoven an 'outrage'. The *Symphonia domestica* made a strong musical impression on Rolland: 'One is dazzled by the beauty of this light, soft, compliant, subtle orchestra, particularly after the compact orchestral mass of Mahler, that heavy bread that has not risen. . . .'[64]

The programme of the *Symphonia domestica*, however, Rolland did not accept, calling it one of the most audacious challenges that Strauss had 'hurled at taste and common-sense'.[65]

Strauss confessed in a letter to Rolland written a few weeks after the Alsatian Musical Festival that Mahler had said something similar to him: 'You may be right about the programme of the *Domestica*. You are entirely in agreement with G. Mahler, who utterly condemns the programme.'[66]

A few days after the Musical Festival in Strasbourg, the annual gathering of the Allgemeiner Deutscher Musikverein took place. The host town on this occasion was Austrian. In June 1903 Strauss had written to his friend and colleague Max von Schillings: '. . . I think Graz excellent . . . and I believe that Graz is very good soil for us in contrast to the very backward Vienna. . . . So let it be Graz. But at any rate Mahler must give us one or two Festival operas on the way there and back.'[67]

Mahler's contribution to the Graz Musical Festival consisted of a series of songs—*Kindertotenlieder* and other settings of Rückert, songs from *Des Knaben Wunderhorn*—and he corresponded intensively with Strauss on the place and timing of their performance (pp. 77–80). Strauss passed through Vienna at the end of May and travelled with Mahler to Graz, probably on 30 May 1905. Mahler reports on this journey to his wife: 'I was quite alone in a coupé with Strauss from Vienna to Graz and we talked very agreeably

Rivalry and Friendship

as in the old days. Unfortunately he was called away the next day by the sudden death of his (84-year-old) father and did not hear my songs.'[68]

Following on the Graz Festival Mahler offered the participants three performances at the Vienna Opera: *Feuersnot* by Strauss, *Die Rose vom Liebesgarten* by Pfitzner and *Die Legende von der heiligen Elisabeth* by Liszt. Max von Schillings, after Strauss the most influential man in the Allgemeiner Deutscher Musikverein, who had reservations regarding Mahler, was enthusiastic about these Festival performances and sent a report to that effect to Strauss.

While still in Strasbourg Strauss had played Mahler and his wife the not yet quite complete *Salome* on the piano. We know of this only from the recollections of Alma Mahler who, as many examples show, was often very free with dates and facts. Surprisingly Strauss, about whom Alma Mahler had served up a trivial, scandalous anecdote a few pages earlier, fares extremely well on this occasion. His effect must have been irresistible; this is felt even from Alma's somewhat spiteful report.

Strauss was cheerful and communicative at that time. His *Salome* was finished. He asked Mahler whether he would like to hear him play the opera from the manuscript. This had a minor antecedent. When Strauss had told Mahler that he wanted to put Wilde's *Salome* to music, Mahler opposed the idea violently. He had a thousand arguments against it, ethical to begin with but not least the probable impossibility of performing the work in Catholic countries. Strauss disagreed and was irritated, though not for long. I told Mahler afterwards that I was surprised he should want to talk Strauss out of setting a particular libretto. It was like advising a man not to marry the woman he loved.

So now Strauss had finished the composition, and there was a note of triumph in his offer. He had located a piano shop and the three of us made our way to the place, where there were dozens of pianos. The room had big gleaming windows on all sides, with people constantly walking past or stopping to look in — pressing their noses against the window as they tried to catch the sound.

Strauss played and sang incomparably well. Mahler was enthralled. We came to the dance. It was missing. 'I haven't done that yet!' said Strauss and after this big hiatus played on to the end. Mahler asked, 'Isn't it risky simply to leave out the dance and do it later when one is no longer in the mood of the work?' But Strauss laughed in his carefree way, 'I'll manage.' But he did not, for the dance is the only weak thing in the

Fig. 2   Strauss, silhouette by Hans Schliessmann.

score—a mere compilation of the commonplace. Mahler was entirely won over. One can risk anything if one has the genius to make the preposterous plausible.[69]

In contrast to the 'eighties and the 'nineties, when opera houses had new works like *The Bartered Bride, Cavalleria Rusticana, Falstaff, Pique Dame* or *La Bohème* at their disposal, in the new century a certain stagnation made itself felt. Mahler had rehearsed many new works at the Court Opera but hardly a single one that had run for any length of time. That he recognized the dramatic power and the historic musical rank of *Salome* at once in Strasbourg, when Strauss gave a foretaste of the score, singing at the piano, must be doubted, but on his return to Vienna he spoke of it with enthusiasm, to his superiors among others, and wanted to perform the new work as soon as possible. While he anticipated difficulties with the censor, he thought they would be surmountable. This censorship did not extend to the whole of Austrian theatrical life but was limited to the Court Theatre. The theatres maintained by the Emperor were not to perform anything that disseminated subversive or lascivious ideas, and above all no words should be let fall that might offend the religious sentiments of the audience. The censor had also made difficulties before the Vienna performance of *Feuersnot* (pp. 56, 58–9 and 60), but these were removed by the first performance at the Court Theatre in Dresden. At that time the General Intendant had written to Mahler: 'The success of the première [in Dresden], and particularly its critical reception, will fundamentally influence the decision on the performance of this opera at the Court Theatre here. . . .'[70]

Mahler was counting on being able to perform *Salome* too after some conflict with the censor, provided the first performance at Dresden was free of scandal. He was wrong. In *Feuersnot* the point at issue had been an indecent joke: the censor had not wished to appear prudish and had turned a blind eye; with *Salome*, the text of which was by the socially ostracized Oscar Wilde, the criteria were different. The censor objected not only to a subject which 'belonged to the sphere of sexual pathology', but still more to the corporeal appearance of John the Baptist and his allusions to Jesus Christ.[71] The battle with the censor can be exactly reconstructed from the correspondence between Mahler and Strauss (pp. 82–95). There is no argument, no tactic that Mahler did not make use of. He extolled the opera, that he knew only from the vocal score, as a modern masterpiece; he warned that the Vienna Volksoper would steal a march on the Court Opera; he thought of textual changes to appease the censor; he helped to bring about a

Rivalry and Friendship

guest performance by the Breslau Opera, who were to show *Salome* in Vienna to make his opponents 'see reason'.

Although all this was in vain—probably because an archduchess opposed the scheme—Mahler never gave up. The battle ended only with his resignation. In one of his letters to Strauss he spoke of raising, in the extreme case, the 'question of confidence', of making his staying at the Vienna Opera dependent on the acceptance of *Salome* (p. 92). Strauss urged him not to do so (p. 93) and Mahler followed his advice. Nevertheless the *Salome* affair, that started in autumn 1905 and continued to smoulder in 1906, influenced Mahler's resignation in spring 1907. He did not resign because of the ban on *Salome*, or at least not only because of it, yet his powerlessness before the censor undoubtedly heightened his disenchantment with the theatre, his latent weariness of directing. 'We know that his departure was decided in his own mind,' writes Richard Specht, an early biographer of Mahler who also wrote a monograph on Strauss, 'once he was unable to win admission to the Court Opera for *Salome*, he felt he was in the wrong place if his powers did not permit him to produce the most fascinating work of his time in the institution he led.'[72]

At the height of the *Salome* affair, on 7 and 8 November 1905, while in Berlin to hear a performance of his Second Symphony under Oscar Fried, Mahler had an opportunity to discuss with Strauss how to proceed *vis-à-vis* his Intendant and censor. Unfortunately he did not report their decisions to his wife, but merely passed on his observations on the Strauss household, which was clearly a constant topic of discussion for the Mahlers.

> It was quite pleasant at the Strauss's yesterday; but he always puts on a certain blasé coolness. Incidentally, he presented me with his latest publication (a Berlioz treatise on instrumentation with dressing of his own), which you will find very interesting and instructive. I shall give it to you for your library; he also promised me a score of *Salome*, which I likewise dedicate to you so that the envy of all creative musicians can henceforth reach fever pitch. But, as I said, I should have preferred a little more warmth to all that.[73]

Surprisingly, Mahler did not go to Dresden for the first performance of *Salome*. Although he set such store by warmth, he seems to have overlooked the possibility that Strauss might take his absence to mean indifference. When—about a year later—Strauss did not appear at the Berlin performance of his Third Symphony (see pp. 148), Mahler was offended, although Strauss had written him an extremely friendly card to apologize.

Rivalry and Friendship

He does not seem to have sent a card to Dresden to explain his staying away, for Strauss asked slightly reproachfully on 15 December 1905 (p. 90), 'Where were you on the 9th? I missed you *very much*.' Like many oversensitive people, Mahler may have judged Strauss's behaviour by a different standard from his own.

Mahler saw *Salome* for the first time on 16 May 1906 in Graz ('an excellent soil ... unlike the very backward Vienna', Strauss wrote in a different connection), where the composer conducted the first three performances. According to Alma Mahler's recollection Strauss waited for them at the hotel and took them on a motor excursion the afternoon before the Graz première. They stopped at a small inn where they soon felt so comfortable that despite the advancing hour Strauss was reluctant to leave.

> Finally, when it was beginning to grow cool and dusk was falling, Mahler got up and said, 'All right, if you are not coming I shall go and conduct for you.' That helped. Strauss slowly got up and while Mahler urged the chauffeur to hurry Strauss restrained him—Mahler seemed to have the authorial nerves that Strauss lacked, but perhaps Strauss was not as calm as he wanted us to believe; perhaps he was very agitated and was hiding it behind his flippancy. [When the 82-year-old Richard Strauss read this last sentence, he wrote in the margin, 'All untrue.' He underlined and wrote 'No' against Alma's surmise that he was hiding his nervousness.] The morning after the performance, which had been a great success although we had feared Christian–Social scandals, Strauss came up to us at breakfast and began reproaching Mahler for taking everything, e.g. the [Vienna] Opera—that farmyard—too seriously; he should look after himself better. No one would give him anything for wearing himself out. A pigsty that would not even put on *Salome*—no, it was not worth it![74]

By way of exception, Alma Mahler endorses Strauss's words. Regrettably she does not report this conversation in the same detail as many trivial ones where she can put Strauss in the wrong. The exact course of the discussion would have been interesting because we must assume that Strauss's exhortation that he should look after his health was not entirely without effect on Mahler. Strauss regarded his own activity at the Berlin Opera as a means of livelihood that allowed him the luxury of composing. Some years before, he had admitted to his parents that he had no wish to conduct operas for ten months a year until he was sixty, and that he would give up Berlin immediately if he could find a better paid post.[75] The

Rivalry and Friendship

unprecedented success of *Salome* brought his goal—to conduct less and compose more—unexpectedly closer. Mahler, the vacation composer, who groaned for ten months a year under the weight of opera management, had until recently been wholeheartedly devoted to this loved-and-hated institution. If he was now growing aloof from the Vienna Opera, there were three main reasons: the realization that it was impossible to keep a repertory theatre at the highest standard day after day; the banning of *Salome*; and the increasingly frequent invitations to go on concert tours conducting his own works. In this situation, and almost a year before his resignation, Strauss's admonitions, whatever their form, must have given him pause. Perhaps it was on this occasion that, in agreeing, he coined his dictum: 'Strauss and I are digging our tunnels from different sides of the same mountain. We shall surely meet some day.'[76] Alma Mahler, at any rate, places these words, used by Mahler for the first time in the letter to Arthur Seidl, in this context.

A few days after the Graz meeting Strauss and Mahler saw each other again, this time at the Festival of the Allgemeiner Deutscher Musikverein in Essen. Mahler had been invited to rehearse the first performance of his Sixth Symphony, that difficult, confessional work that most strongly expresses his personality and anticipates his death. Accompanying Mahler was a young man from a good Munich family named Klaus Pringsheim, who worked as a répétiteur at the Vienna Opera. From him we have a report on the rehearsals and on Mahler's relationship to Strauss at that time.

> ... he builds, piles peak upon peak and so arises, overwhelming, gigantic, in masses that Mahler had never dared to accumulate before and in truth was never to do again, the last movement.
>
> After the rehearsal Richard Strauss remarked, in his nonchalant way, that the movement was 'over-instrumented'—the Strauss of the *Salome* score. (It was a great year for German music, that brought us *Salome* and Mahler's Sixth.) Over-instrumented? The word made Mahler thoughtful. (Because Strauss had said it.) He kept coming back to it, talked much about his relationship to Strauss.—He spoke, as always, in a movingly human way, and everyone listened to him as to a sage; for Mahler taught as Socrates taught: in conversation he gave, without any appearance of giving, unstintingly.—He spoke not of himself but of the other, whom he had never failed to recognize, asked without envy, without bitterness, almost humbly, reverently, what might be the reason why everything came so easily to that other, and so painfully to himself; and one felt the

antithesis between the blond conqueror and the dark, fate-burdened man....[77]

Three years previously a short story had appeared that, in a vivid metaphor, presented this antithesis of fair haired nonchalance and dark sensitivity—*Tonio Kröger* by Thomas Mann. Klaus Pringsheim undoubtedly knew this work, for everyone was talking about it and its author happened to be his brother-in-law. So it is not surprising that this répétiteur versed in literature as well as music should have compared his director to Tonio, who loved, and suffered through loving. It may be that, clairvoyant as sensitive young people are apt to be, he fathomed Mahler's relationship to Strauss more deeply, through his literary allusion, than all other observers.

Mahler himself repeatedly stressed the artistic differences between himself and Strauss, not least in his symphonies, which since 1901 had dispensed with programmes and even with words set to music. But since Mahler had begun expressing his ideas only in musical and symphonic terms, he had become increasingly self-critical with regard to instrumentation. None of his works was so often and extensively revised as the Fifth Symphony, the first to do without text or human voices after the three *Wunderhorn* symphonies. His emancipation from the literary clearly awakened in him higher demands on orchestration in the service of expression and clarity. Perhaps this incessant struggle to be understood—his 'dissatisfaction with himself' as Pringsheim called it—made his inner dependence on Strauss's judgement stronger than ever.

In this connection... Mahler said something which probably implied far more than was explicitly stated. It is strange, he said, that Strauss needs only a few rehearsals, yet the music always 'sounds right'; whereas he, Mahler, toils with the orchestra in countless rehearsals to bring out everything as he wants it—but when could he really say after a performance that nothing was lacking?[78]

This feeling of insecurity and of being at a disadvantage that accompanied the three instrumental symphonies and probably disappeared with the Eighth, might explain why it was precisely in these years that Strauss played such an important role in Mahler's thinking and feeling, why Mahler observed and commented on each of Strauss's words and gestures, and complained constantly of his coolness. Mahler envied him, even though—like Tonio Kröger—he undoubtedly never felt the wish to be like him, longing only for agreement and admiration.

Rivalry and Friendship

Even Alma Mahler perceived the special position Strauss occupied for her husband, even if she never acknowledged it. When she came to the final rehearsals in Essen, she found Mahler surrounded by admirers, by Ossip Gabrilovich, Oscar Fried and Klaus Pringsheim, who were later joined by Willem Mengelberg. And at this juncture we find her making this surprising admission: 'The only one who still mattered for Mahler was Strauss, beside him all the rest were more or less insignificant.'[79]

This observation of Alma Mahler's accords so exactly with Pringsheim's reports that we must take it as accurate. Her other comments from Essen must be viewed with scepticism, as, for example, nothing is known of a Vienna performance of the Second Symphony at this time. Nevertheless, two extracts from her memoirs will be quoted here, primarily because Strauss read and annotated them, so that, from these marginal notes, we can ascertain at least his later attitude to Mahler.

> The day of our arrival in Essen we had met Strauss in the street. Just before, Mahler had had a great success in Vienna with the Second, that had to be repeated. Strauss came up to him and called out. 'Well, you Viennese celebrity, how are you?' We were so taken aback that we walked on without a word. We afterwards saw Strauss often from a distance, but kept out of his way.[80]

Beside this passage Strauss wrote in 1946, 'I was always glad when Mahler had successes.' Three paragraphs before, Alma Mahler gives an account of a scene during preparations for the first performance of the Sixth Symphony.

> The final rehearsals! The last movement of the work with the three great strokes of fate. No work affected him so much when he first heard it. After the full rehearsal Mahler paced up and down in the dressing room, sobbing, wringing his hands, unable to control himself. Fried, Gabrilovich, Buths and I stood silent and petrified, no one daring to look at the others. Strauss suddenly came noisily in, noticing nothing. 'Mahler, you'll have to conduct a funeral overture or something of the sort tomorrow before the Sixth—the mayor has died. It's the done thing—well, whatever is the matter with you? What is going on? Ah, well!—' And he went out, blustering and coldhearted, leaving us benumbed behind him.

This time Strauss wrote in the margin, 'I don't pretend to understand such things.'

Rivalry and Friendship

Many letters written by Mahler to his wife in these years reveal his need to be understood more deeply by Strauss.

> But, as I said, I should have preferred a little more warmth to all that. [November 1905 from Berlin][81]
>
> You can feel the coldness in Strauss's nature, that comes not from his talent but from the human side, and it repels you. [May 1906 from Essen][82]
>
> Strauss is constantly here, and very friendly, as always when he is alone with me. But his nature will always be alien to me. His way of thinking and feeling is worlds apart from mine. Shall we ever meet again on the same star? [August 1906 from Salzburg][83]

The relationship presents itself quite differently from Strauss's viewpoint. He, too, mentions Mahler in his letters, but matter-of-factly and dispassionately, though with perceptible goodwill and respect.

> I learned with great pleasure that you too have now joined in the just and, I hope, profitable efforts of our Genossenschaft. ... And I was also very pleased that you have acquired the new symphony by my friend Mahler. ... [To the publisher, C. F. Peters][84]
>
> Have you read Arthur Seidl in the Berlin *Neueste Nachrichten*? Enjoyed it immensely, I expect? Now it's not just you he is after, but the powers that be, who wouldn't perform a two-hour Mahler symphony because they fear 'being overshadowed' (me by Mahler!). [To Max von Schillings. Strauss, himself one of the 'powers that be', was irritated by Seidl's suggestion that he had blocked a Mahler performance.][85]
>
> Invite Mahler, at any rate. He conducts Beethoven very interestingly. The shortest (one hour) of his symphonies is No. IV, G major (without chorus or trombone). [To Friedrich Sieger][86]
>
> This afternoon, rehearsals with the Vienna Philharmonic, tomorrow, Thursday, at 3 p.m., public final rehearsal. On Sunday Mahler conducts *Figaro* here. So it would be very nice if you could come as soon as possible. ... [To Pauline Strauss][87]
>
> I am, unfortunately, one of those people who, when artistic interests are at stake, do not ask themselves whether there might be a collision of personal interest. ... Just as even now I learn like a schoolboy from you and Mahler and everyone who has ability, without wondering whether this might move my pedestal from its proper place. ... [To Ernst von Schuch][88]

Rivalry and Friendship

Two-and-a-half months after the encounter in Essen, Strauss and Mahler met in Salzburg. In mid-August 1906 Mozart's 150th anniversary was celebrated with opera performances and concerts—it was the Salzburg Festspiele, though it did not yet bear that name. The new Vienna production of *Le Nozze di Figaro*, with scenery by Alfred Roller, travelled for the occasion to Salzburg, and Mahler interrupted his vacation at the Wörthersee to conduct the performance. Strauss's participation had not been planned, but arose from the sudden illness of Carl Muck, in whose place Strauss conducted the second orchestral concert.

Little time had passed since the meeting in Essen, yet much had happened in the interval. Strauss had begun to set Hugo von Hofmannsthal's *Elektra* to music; Mahler had composed his Eighth Symphony, and both were full of their creative experiences. From Mahler's letters to his wife, who had stayed at the Wörthersee, we know that Strauss and Mahler were constantly together during the days in Salzburg, and that it was Strauss who sought Mahler's company. From the frequent mentions of *Elektra* we may conclude that Strauss talked much of his new opera, and from the way Mahler reports on it we must assume that he rejected the subject as strongly as he had earlier opposed that of *Salome*. His literary taste, as we can also see from the poems he set to music, was thoroughly conservative. He never applied solely aesthetic standards to what he read, but above all ethical ones. He did not know what to make of the works of the modern Austrian writers, Hugo von Hofmannsthal, Hermann Bahr or Arthur Schnitzler, who were all his admirers. They were doubtless too 'decadent' for him and he disapproved of Strauss's predilection for such tendencies. Only this can explain his mocking characterization of a journalist living in Paris: 'He gives an impression of such highly intellectual perversity. Perhaps Strauss will set him to music one day.'[89]

In one of his notebooks Strauss recalls that he played from *Elektra* on the piano to Mahler. However, this is more likely to have happened in the winter of 1906–7, when the composition was further advanced. In Salzburg, the opera was probably only talked about, and Strauss's enthusiasm for his new work was such that he tried to persuade Mahler to write an opera as well. In his rapture he neglected to ask what Mahler had composed that summer, and Mahler, in his reserve, exactly like Tonio Kröger, forbore to mention it first. His new symphony, the Eighth, was a vocal symphony, the first part of which was based on the Latin hymn 'Veni creator spiritus', and the second on the closing scene of *Faust* Part II. How remote this was from Hofmannsthal and *Elektra*! Mahler, clearly offended at being unable to speak of his symphony, armed himself with irony and a touch of arrogance.

> Strauss has already composed a number of scenes from *Elektra* (Hofmannsthal). He won't part with it for less than 10 per cent per evening and 100,000 marks. (That is just my guess, I admit.) As he did not inquire, I did not tell him anything about my antiquated existence this summer. I doubt whether he would be much impressed to hear with what quaint relics I occupy my summer. Oh, how blissful to be modern.[90]

In the same year, 1906, when Mahler's feelings towards his friend and rival manifested themselves more ambivalently, almost, than at any time before, there occurred a conversation about Strauss between Mahler and the composer Bernard Scharlitt. Scharlitt claims to have taken notes on the conversation and later reproduced it, 'much abbreviated'. We must regret this abbreviation, for it would not have been without importance to know whether Mahler, by his polarization of the 'timely' and the 'untimely', was describing solely musical qualities, or whether a divergent approach to literature also played a part. Scharlitt attributes the following statement to Mahler:

> Only when I have shaken the dust of the earth from me will justice be done to me. For, to speak with Nietzsche, I am an 'untimely' person, a man 'out of season'. This is connected, above all, to the nature of my creation. The truly 'timely' one is Richard Strauss. That is why he enjoys immortality while still on earth. Also, I value his musical-dramatic creation more highly that his symphonic work and I believe posterity will do likewise.[91]

By 'musical-dramatic creation' Mahler can at this time only have meant *Salome*, since *Elektra* was not yet finished, and he was certainly not among those who overestimated *Guntram* and *Feuersnot*. Even his appraisal of *Salome* fluctuated before he saw the work in the Berlin performance. Until then he was not sure whether it was a masterpiece or just a virtuoso work. In December 1906 Strauss came to Vienna where he conducted the Philharmonic, which he had got to know in Salzburg, in a concert on the 16th. According to his diary he was invited to lunch with Mahler on that day. A few weeks later Mahler went to Berlin to conduct his Third Symphony at a Philharmonic concert. Six letters to Alma about this Berlin visit have been preserved, in which Strauss plays a predominant part. The meetings with

Rivalry and Friendship

him, or rather the resultant emotions, even pervade two letters Mahler wrote from Frankfurt where his tour took him immediately afterwards. In one of the Berlin letters Mahler, against his usual practice and obviously to affirm Alma's views on Pauline Strauss, writes at length on the reception he was given.

> Yesterday afternoon I was at Strauss's. She met me at the door saying: Hush, Richard is asleep, pulled me into her (very untidy) boudoir, where her old Mamma was drinking Kaffe (not Kaffee) and inundated me with gossip about all the financial and sexual happenings of the last two years, interspersed hastily with questions about 'a thousand and one' things without waiting for an answer; she flatly refused to let me go, told me that yesterday morning Richard had had an exhausting rehearsal in Leipzig, then had come back to Berlin to conduct the *Götterdämmerung* in the evening, and this afternoon, completely worn out, was lying down while she diligently guarded his sleep. I was quite touched. Suddenly she jumped up: Now the rascal must wake up. Unable to stop her, I was dragged by both fists into the room while she intoned in a stentorian voice: Up you get! Gustav is here! (For an hour I was Gustav—then suddenly Herr Direktor once again). Strauss sat up, smiled in a long-suffering way, and the three of us went busily back to our gossip. Then we had tea and they brought me back to the hotel by car, after we had arranged that I should have lunch with them on Saturday....[92]

The lunch to which he was invited was not described at similar length by Mahler, as a 'detailed description ... stuck in my throat'. He was clearly offended or jealous because the conductor Leo Blech was also invited.

> ... and as he (Richard) divides the sunlight of his favour so absent-mindedly and conventionally between me and Blech, the friendly and respectful concern I show for him on such occasions is scattered to the winds, without an echo and probably without even being noticed.—I am totally at a loss with myself and the world when this happens to me over and over again! Are people made of different stuff than I?[93]

Strauss answered this question by a single word in the margin: 'Yes'. He was doubtless right; they were made of different stuff, and the stuff that Strauss was made of contained too much healthy naturalness for him to discern from Mahler's contradictory judgements that, for him, an amiability shared with Leo Blech was not enough, that he wanted more, friendship, affection. Mahler stressed several times in his letters that Strauss

Rivalry and Friendship

was 'very kind' as soon as they were alone. But it never seems to have occurred to him to infer Strauss's special affection from this observation. The day after the desperate letter in which Mahler was at a loss with himself, Strauss and the world, he shows himself contented again.

> By the way, I met Strauss before the performance in the Opera House—he was again (alone) very kind and insisted on being with me afterwards. We met, he, his wife and mother-in-law ... in a restaurant and talked about everything in a very friendly and searching way. It was all most enjoyable, apart from the high-spirited intermezzi from the 'eternal feminine'.[94]

But it did not end there either, for Strauss stayed away from Mahler's concert, excusing himself, it is true, with a very flattering card (p. 96). Mahler was offended—we can take him at his word—but consoled himself by blaming Strauss's absence on Pauline: 'It was hurtful to me that Strauss was not at the concert. When I got back, I found the enclosed card; most probably, as I now understand it, Frau Pauline would not let him go!'[95]

More important than these emotional irritations, however, were the two performances of *Salome* that Mahler saw in Berlin and which firmly decided his previously wavering opinion of the work. Mahler attended the performance of 9 January 1907 conducted by Leo Blech, and the performance on 12 January when Strauss himself was on the rostrum. After the first performance he wrote Alma the lines already quoted in part, in which he revised the image he had formed of Strauss and felt happy because of it.

> It is a work of genius, very powerful, decidedly one of the most important that our time has produced! Deeply at work in it, under a mass of rubble, is a live volcano, a subterranean fire—not a mere firework! It is probably the same with Strauss's whole personality! That is what makes it so hard to separate the wheat from the chaff in him. But I have enormous respect for the phenomenon as a whole, and have now reaffirmed it. I am immensely glad. This I can approve entirely! Yesterday Blech conducted (admirably). On Saturday Strauss is conducting and I am going again![96]

And on 13 January 1907 Mahler wrote to his wife about the performance conducted by Strauss himself.

> So yesterday it was *Salome*! I had an even stronger impression, and I am firmly convinced that this is one of the greatest masterpieces of our

Rivalry and Friendship

time.—I cannot explain it to myself, and can only surmise that from within genius speaks the voice of the 'Earth Spirit', who does not choose his abode according to human taste but builds it according to his own unfathomable needs. Perhaps time will give me a better understanding of this 'receptacle'![97]

Mahler was not granted the time to understand Strauss better. When he returned from the concert tour of January 1907 that took him to Berlin and Frankfurt, the newspaper campaign that was to lead a few months later to his resignation as Director of the Court Opera was already raging. Mahler did go twice more to Berlin that year, but on both occasions his stay was so short that it is doubtful whether he even saw Strauss. From the whole of 1907—a fateful year for Mahler—only two letters to Strauss have been preserved. In one of them (p. 96) he recommended Schoenberg's String Quartet Op. 7 for performance at the next Musikverein Festival, in the second he interceded on behalf of his chief set designer Alfred Roller.

Mahler resigned of his own free will. He had had enough. Enough of the immense burden of work and responsibility, enough of the malicious newspapers, enough of the censorship. A few weeks after this decision, which he took of his own accord but which nevertheless left a wound, he was dealt another blow. The first-born of his two little daughters died of diphtheria when she was not yet five. A few days later a heart condition was diagnosed in Mahler. These three hammer-blows changed not only his outlook and mood but his material existence. The man who boarded a ship to America in December 1907 and conducted *Tristan und Isolde* in New York in January 1908, was not the same irritable artist who a year previously had wrestled with the problem of Strauss.

We can therefore suppose that Mahler's strange preoccupation with Strauss reached its climax and its end in 1907; at least there are no documents that prove it continued. For two seasons Mahler conducted at the Metropolitan Opera in New York, though he declined an offer to become Director of that institution. From 1909 to 1911 we find him as conductor of the New York Philharmonic Orchestra. He spent six or seven months of the year in Europe, both conducting his own music, and, above all, in order to have more time than he had had earlier to write his own works. Although he undoubtedly gave of his best as opera and concert conductor in America, he was free of the fanatical perfectionism that had characterized him as Director of the Vienna Opera. His aim was to take major exertions on himself for a number of years so that he could retire in comfort and devote himself entirely to composing. These were, properly considered, Straussian maxims, though ones at which Mahler and his wife had turned up their noses when they were proclaimed by Strauss or even by Frau Pauline. In a letter from New York to his old friend, the musicologist Guido Adler, Mahler described and defended this mode of life à la Strauss.

> I often lie down after rehearsals (I first heard of this regime from Richard Strauss) because I find it wonderfully restorative. In Vienna I just did not have time for such things.—I have very much to do, but not nearly as much as in Vienna. All in all I feel better and fresher working and living like this than I have for many years....
>
> I have an absolute need to exercise my musical faculties practically to counterbalance the enormous inner strain of composition: and all my life I have wanted to conduct a concert orchestra. I am glad to be able to enjoy this once in my life (apart from the fact that I am learning from it; for the technique of the theatre is quite different, and I am convinced that a large number of my previous deficiencies in instrumentation resulted from my being used to hearing the quite different acoustics of the theatre).... Moreover, I need a certain degree of luxury, a comfortable mode of life that my pension (the only one I could obtain after almost thirty years of conducting) would not have permitted. It was therefore a welcome way out for me when America provided not only an activity adequate to my faculties and inclinations, but also an ample recompense that will soon enable me to enjoy the evening of my life in a manner fitting to human beings....[98]

The name of Strauss, although mentioned only once, underlies the subsequent parts of the letter, as it does the comment on instrumentation and theatre acoustics. Moreover, Mahler performed very many works by Strauss with his American orchestra. In the two winters during which he conducted the Philharmonic Orchestra, he performed *Till Eulenspiegel*, *Tod und Verklärung*, *Don Juan*, the *Guntram* Preludes, *Ein Heldenleben*, *Also sprach Zarathustra* and two songs.

As of old, Strauss was slightly ahead of Mahler. The success of *Salome*, that in a very short time was performed at all the major opera houses of the world except the Vienna Court Opera, and the income resulting from it, allowed Strauss to terminate his contract with the Berlin Opera in 1909. He committed himself only to conducting a number of opera evenings and to attending to the concerts of the Königliche Kapelle, a concert orchestra consisting mostly of Berlin Opera players, that he had taken over a year

Rivalry and Friendship

previously. On 19 January 1909 he performed Mahler's Fourth Symphony with this orchestra, and on 3 December 1909 the First Symphony. Up to then a 'vacation composer' like Mahler, Strauss now had time at his disposal, and wrote his opera scores in his study in the Garmisch villa that he had had built from the revenue from *Salome*. When he composed *Elektra* he was still overburdened with opera work, and had to ask for leave of absence to complete the work. More than two years separated the beginning of the work from its completion. He was able to complete the larger score of *Rosenkavalier* in seventeen months.

Of Mahler's attitude to *Elektra* we know little. Many years later Strauss noted in one of his diaries: 'My boldest passage harmonically is perhaps Clytemnestra's day-dream narrative where the pedal-note has the function of nightmare. A piece which even Mahler (it was the last thing I played to him) could not accept.'[99]

This could have taken place in December 1906 in Vienna or in January 1907 in Berlin. Possibly, however, there were one or more personal meetings between Mahler and Strauss between January 1907 and the summer of 1909, when Mahler became acquainted with *Elektra*. The Vienna Court Opera put on a performance of *Elektra* shortly after its Dresden première, but Mahler, though undoubtedly interested, did not see it. After his official departure he never again set foot in the opera house where he had for ten years been Director. According to Alma Mahler's book he first saw *Elektra* the following season in the Manhattan Opera House in New York. 'This opera so displeased Mahler that he wanted to leave in the middle of the performance. We stayed, and agreed afterwards that we had seldom been so bored. The audience decided otherwise.'[100]

In August 1909 the Strauss family left Garmisch, where it was raining, on an automobile tour to the South Tyrol, and took the opportunity to visit Mahler at his vacation address in Toblach (p. 98). Alma Mahler devotes more than a page of her book to this visit. But she recalls only the utterances of Frau Pauline and does not waste a word on Richard Strauss and the conversations that took place. In a letter of September 1909, Mahler refers to this summer meeting, regretting that it was so short, 'almost as between potentates'.

They were indeed two potentates of music. The days when Mahler depended on Strauss's intercession at the Allgemeiner Deutscher Musikverein were past. The preparations had already begun for the first performance of the Eighth Symphony, that took place in the New Exhibition Hall in Munich in September 1910. A few months previously there had been a

Rivalry and Friendship

Richard Strauss week in the same hall. In New York Mahler was busy preparing the parts for the performance of the Eighth Symphony. When he had corrected the vocal score, he sent it to his Vienna publisher together with a list of names, asking him to send each of the gentlemen listed a copy of the score as soon as it was printed. At the head of the list, that contained fourteen names in all, was 'Generalmusikdir. Dr Strauss',[101] in Mahler's mind always the first.

Strauss was among the numerous prominent guests who attended the first performance of the Eighth Symphony on 12 September 1910. Whether he was able to exchange more than a few words with Mahler on this occasion is not known. Nor do we know what impression this work, which the concert organizer called the 'Symphony of a Thousand', made on Strauss.

In honour of Mahler's fiftieth birthday in July 1910, the Vienna musicologist Paul Stefan, an admirer of Mahler and one of his earliest biographers, prepared a publication to which Richard Strauss contributed a few lines. His dedication is brief, but evinces the highest respect. The last sentence in particular must have given pleasure to Mahler, since he had for many years felt uncertain—and Strauss's inferior—in the art of orchestration.

> Gustav Mahler's work is in my view among the most significant and interesting in present-day art history. Just as I was fortunate to be one of the first to commend his symphonic works to the public, I see it as one of my most pleasant duties to continue by word and deed to help his symphonies attain the general recognition they so deserve. The plasticity of his orchestration, in particular, is absolutely exemplary.[102]

In February 1911, in the middle of the New York season, Mahler was taken seriously ill. The American doctors, seeing no prospect of recovery, allowed the patient to be transported to Europe. When Paris medicine likewise failed to find a cure, Mahler, in accordance with his wish, was taken by train to Vienna. The Austrian and German newspapers reported on his stay in Paris and on his journey to Vienna with a minuteness that was reserved for 'potentates'. Strauss must therefore had been fully informed even without direct contacts with Mahler's family. A week before his death he wrote Mahler a letter (p. 100) that reached him in time and of which Alma wrote to Strauss that it had been 'one of Gustav's last joys'. Perhaps Mahler discerned beneath the rather forced cheerfulness of the letter the genuine sympathy for which he had longed for so many years.

Mahler died on 18 May 1911 in Vienna. Strauss noted in his diary:

Rivalry and Friendship

Gustav Mahler after a grave illness ... passed away.

The death of this aspiring, idealistic and energetic artist is a heavy loss. [I] read Wagner's memoirs with emotion. [I] read German history of the age of the Reformation, Leopold Ranke: this confirmed very clearly for me that all the elements that fostered culture at that time have been a spent force for centuries, just as all great political and religious movements can only have a truly fruitful influence for a limited period.

The Jew Mahler could still find elevation in Christianity.

The hero Richard Wagner came back to it as an old man through the influence of Schopenhauer.

It is absolutely clear to me that the German nation can only attain new vigour by freeing itself from Christianity.... I shall call my *Alpensymphonie* the Antichrist, since it embodies: moral purification through one's own strength, liberation through work, worship of eternal, glorious Nature.[103]

When we consider the ideas that passed through Strauss's mind when he heard of Mahler's death, we see in all its clarity what united the two composers and what divided them. Strauss shows himself to be as much under Nietzsche's influence as ever, while Mahler had outgrown it by the turn of the century, if it had ever been a philosophical rather than a merely literary influence. The position derived from Nietzsche is maintained *vis-à-vis* the 'hero' Richard Wagner, whose *Parsifal* had incurred the philosopher's vituperation. Furthermore, Strauss wanted to call his *Alpensymphonie*, on which he was working at the time, the 'Antichrist'—an allusion to Nietzsche's essay criticizing Christianity; from this, however, he abstained. 'What is more harmful than any vice?' asked Nietzsche in his *Antichrist* and answered, 'Active pity for the ill-constituted and weak—Christianity.' Mahler proclaimed such pity, to which he had hardly been converted by the New Testament, however, but by the writings of Dostoyevsky.

Strauss conceded Mahler his adherence to Christianity as a Jew. He clearly saw in Christianity a further and higher development of the older Jewish faith, just as—unlike Nietzsche in this respect—he affirmed the Reformation, that he studied through Ranke, as a culture-promoting force. His opinion that Mahler had found 'elevation' in Christianity may derive from the many conversations the two composers had in the twenty-four years of their acquaintanceship, but it may result simply from his experience of the Eighth Symphony, which Strauss had heard eight months

Rivalry and Friendship

previously. The medieval Latin hymn 'Veni creator spiritus' that forms the first part of the symphony was no doubt rightly interpreted by Strauss as a profession of Christian belief. That this was no narrow, confessional belief is confirmed by the second part of the symphony, in which the final scene of *Faust* Part II is set to music. Even here Catholic voices are heard, but in a framework contrived by a poet who commanded the saints as he did the mythical beings of antiquity, who created his own heaven as he had created his own archetypal devil, and who made his heaven proclaim the law by which he had lived and by which he sought redemption. Mahler too built his own heaven in his symphonies. He interpreted the meaning of life and suffering in sounds, and proclaimed that the resurrection, and the heaven of his Fourth Symphony, which Strauss so valued, was a jubilant, beatific one. A few verses from *Des Knaben Wunderhorn*, a Latin hymn, Goethe's *Faust*, perhaps even the whole of Christian doctrine, served him as building stones for his musical doctrine of redemption.

Thanks to his historical studies, Strauss recognized some years before Oswald Spengler that the great religious and political movements only remain effective for a time and gradually petrify and die. Christianity therefore seemed to him to be ballast the jettisoning of which was a precondition for the new upsurge of the German nation which he hoped for. To himself—and doubtless to the whole nation—he prescribed moral purification through one's own strength, liberation by work, reverence for eternal, glorious Nature. In these three demands he would have come together with Mahler again: indeed, we may suppose that adherence to these maxims—whether tacit or explicit—formed the basis of their mutual respect. Strauss could not yet suspect that the ethical standards he applied to himself would two decades later become slogans of a propaganda wrongfully claiming allegiance to Nietzsche.

Strauss survived Mahler by thirty-eight years, but never forgot him. There were even to be years in which he thought of him daily, since he frequented the rooms in which Mahler had worked, and because he was confronted by the same joys and irritations. In October 1918 *Salome* had finally gained admittance to the Vienna Opera. Some months later, in August 1919, Strauss himself moved into the Director's office at the opera house that was no longer called the Court Opera Theatre but the Vienna State Opera. His co-director was Franz Schalk, whom Mahler had engaged as a conductor, the orchestra was made up of musicians the majority of whom had played under Mahler, and on the stage were still many singers who—according to their degree of insight—had loved or hated Mahler.

Rivalry and Friendship

In the first weeks of his office Strauss was subjected to a similar press campaign to that of Mahler's last year, but he bore it more lightly, as he had the happier temperament and because he had witnessed the spectacle from afar in Mahler's case. Strauss got on better with the Philharmonic than his predecessor. The high point of the amity between composer and orchestra was a South American Tour in the summer of 1923. On this tour Strauss introduced two of Mahler's symphonies to Latin American audiences, his two favourites, the First and the Fourth. Mahler had endured the Vienna Opera for ten years, Strauss stood it for only six. He resigned in the autumn of 1924.

Just as Strauss was composing the score for *Die schweigsame Frau*, the libretto of which had been written for him by a Jewish writer from Austria, Stefan Zweig, Hitler seized power, in January 1933. Strauss had been active in the German Empire, in Republican Germany, and in the Austrian Republic; his operas and orchestral works were played throughout the world. Governments came and went, he may have thought; what remained was art. When, in mid-November 1933, he was appointed President of the Reichsmusikkammer, he accepted the office. Perhaps he allowed himself to be taken in by the new men in power, perhaps he hoped by his reputation to promote good and avert evil within his sphere of influence. Perhaps he was, after all, somewhat unworldly despite his apparent sophistication. This seems the only interpretation admitted by Strauss's letter of 13 December 1933 to the conductor Wilhelm Furtwängler, a naïve letter proving that Strauss remained true to himself even in Hitler's Germany, even in his attitude towards Mahler.

> Geheimrat Spiess has just written to tell me that a Frankfurt district administrator of culture has protested at a performance of Debussy's *Nocturne* at a Museum Concert and has written to Dr Benecke. While Herr Minister Goebbels recently instructed me to report any interference by provincial Caesars of that kind directly to him, I hardly think that necessary, since you are the highest authority with regard to concert programmes. Would you kindly write to inform Herr Geheimrat Spiess that the *Nocturne* is no more objectionable than a Mahler symphony, which he has not yet dared to put on to the programme. Perhaps you could also see to it that any further interference by this cultural official in the Museum's choice of programme is forbidden....[104]

Strauss could not, of course, bring about a performance of a Mahler symphony in the Third Reich. That he managed a first performance of *Die schweigsame Frau* with Zweig's name on the playbill was a considerable achievement. The result was that he was soon being urged to resign as President of the Reichsmusikkammer.

In the spring of 1938 Austria was annexed. Among the refugees was Alma Mahler, now married for the third time (to the writer Franz Werfel). From Paris, where she first took refuge, she went to Holland to attend the Mahler performances conducted by Willem Mengelberg. Amsterdam, where she was honoured as the composer's consort, seemed to Alma a peaceful paradise. She was interviewed over and over again until finally a representative of the Dutch publishing house Allert de Lange called to offer her a contract for a book on Mahler. According to Alma this book had long been written and had only to be edited for publication.

Among the papers of Alma Mahler preserved at the University of Pennsylvania there is a copy of a typescript with numerous handwritten addenda and corrections bearing the title *Ein Leben mit Gustav Mahler*. It is an earlier version of the book *Gustav Mahler. Erinnerungen und Briefe* (*Gustav Mahler: Memories and Letters*, see p. 159) that came out in 1940 in Amsterdam. Like the published edition, the typescript is divided into two sections. Alma's recollections and Mahler's letters to her. Scattered throughout the letter section we find letters from various people to Mahler. Alma's original intention was to include several letters by Strauss, for the typescript contains transcripts of no less than twelve letters addressed by Strauss to Mahler between 1904 and 1909. In the summer of 1939 she appears to have approached Strauss with a request for permission to publish these letters. She received a negative reply.

The papers she left behind include the following letter in Strauss's handwriting.

9 August 1939

Dear Frau Mahler

Forgive me for not replying sooner, owing to birthday commitments. I hasten to tell you that I cannot allow publication of my letters, even those to dear Gustav. With the exception of my correspondence with Hofmannsthal, which seemed to me an artistic necessity, I have up to now turned down every request to publish my letters (only recently I had to refuse Frau Hermann Bahr), so that for the sake of consistency I cannot fulfil your request, which I am sure you will understand.

Rivalry and Friendship

Otherwise we are well: I'm working on a new opera and hope you and your husband are in good and active health.

With best regards to you both, from Pauline too,

Yours ever
Dr Richard Strauss[105]

This letter appears to have angered Alma Mahler beyond measure, and to have been the immediate occasion of the preface to *Gustav Mahler. Erinnerungen und Briefe* which is dated: 'Sanary sur mer, Summer 1939.' In this preface Alma Mahler affirms that it had not been her original intention to publish this memoir during her lifetime. But now the European world had changed fundamentally. The bust of Mahler by Rodin, which she had donated to the Vienna State Opera, had been removed, the street next to the Opera, once named after Mahler, was now called Meistersingerstrasse, the money collected for a monument to Mahler had been diverted into a National Socialist welfare fund.

I therefore no longer feel myself prohibited from openly reporting experiences with people who are today playing an active role in the Third Reich. The doors between us have been slammed, from both sides. Everything related here about Richard Strauss is based on entries in my diary. One should not forget that this greatest master of contemporary music was in the first decade of this century Gustav Mahler's only rival.[106]

These sentences in the introduction prefigure the book's tendency. It was not only a book about Mahler, but a book against Strauss. To Alma's credit it should be said that the many malicious words about Strauss in the main body of the book were not written in August 1939 under the influence of his refusal. They are already in the typescript clearly written earlier, and in the final revision were moderated rather than intensified. When the book appeared, Strauss had five years previously ceased to be President of the Reichsmusikkammer, but he was composing and conducting, being honoured and fêted, and was installed with his family in the Garmisch villa, while the hero of Alma's book was proscribed as a Jew, and Alma herself, on account of her third husband, was subjected to the rigours of emigration. The political situation gave her invective an apparent justification. Insignificant incidents that had happened thirty years previously took on a false topicality, trivialities that would otherwise have been dismissed as gossip were distorted into accusations. Alma's political preface cast a new light on everything. It was undoubtedly not the right light to illuminate the complex and complicated relationship between Mahler and Strauss.

In the autumn of 1945, soon after the overthrow of the Third Reich, Richard Strauss and his wife sought sanctuary in Switzerland from hunger, cold and the hostility directed at the former President of the Reichsmusikkammer. They stayed for more than three years. In this period Strauss drew up for Bernhard Paumgartner, who was reviving the Salzburg Festspiele, a 'Salzburg List of Composers (including the Saxons Händel and Richard Wagner)' on which the concert programmes were to be based. On this list Mahler was represented by the First and Fourth Symphonies and by *Das Lied von der Erde*.[107]

A few weeks later Strauss came across a copy of Alma's book in the library of his Swiss friend and subsequent biographer Willi Schuh, and set about reading it. A number of his handwritten marginalia on accounts of particular events given by Alma have been quoted elsewhere in this essay. On the flyleaf of the volume Strauss wrote, in understandable indignation, on 28 December 1946, a number of angry words about Alma, from which it emerges that the spiteful characterization of his wife had offended him more than what was directed at him: 'What surprises me in this book that is not especially flattering even to Mahler, whom I much admired as an artist and with whom I had only friendly relations, is that he apparently bore me not the slightest trace of gratitude for introducing him to the public....'

Anyone who knows Alma Mahler's book will agree that Strauss had good reason to be offended. Understandably, what he had just read was more vivid to him than the experiences of many decades previously. His recollection of former conversations, and the cordial letters he had received from Mahler, were eclipsed by a description that was intended to wound and succeeded in doing so. Mahler's letters to Alma published in the volume alternate, when Strauss is their subject, between respect and contempt, affection and dislike. Such feverish fluctuation of the emotions was inevitably incomprehensible to the level-headed Richard Strauss who 'always kept his feet on the ground'.

Alma Mahler could have explained these contradictions but clearly had no such intention. What she wrote, and even more what she omitted, was bound to misrepresent the relationship between Strauss and Mahler. She was aided in this by the fact that the correspondence between the two composers remained unpublished for so long. The documents presented here are intended to place the Mahler–Strauss relationship in a truer light, and so to correct the traditional, distorted image.

Key to Principal Bibliographical Sources

GML   *Selected Letters of Gustav Mahler* edited by Knud Martner, Faber and Faber, London, 1979 (an enlarged English edition of *Gustav Mahler: Briefe 1879–1911* edited by Alma Maria Mahler, Paul Zsolnay Verlag, Vienna, 1924)

AM   *Gustav Mahler. Memories and Letters* edited by Donald Mitchell, the third edition enlarged and with an additional Appendix and Chronology by Knud Martner, Faber and Faber, London, 1973 and Seattle, 1975 (an enlarged edition of *Gustav Mahler. Erinnerungen und Briefe*, Amsterdam, 1940)

RST Briefe   *Der Strom der Töne trug mich fort. Die Welt um Richard Strauss in Briefen* edited by Franz Grasberger in collaboration with Franz and Alice Strauss, Tutzing, 1967

RST Eltern   *Richard Strauss Briefe an die Eltern 1882–1906* edited by Willi Schuh, Zurich, 1954

RST Betrachtungen   *Betrachtungen und Erinnerungen* Richard Strauss, Zurich, 1949

Schuh   *Richard Strauss, Jugend und frühe Meisterjahre* Willi Schuh, Zurich, 1976 (page references are to this German edition, although this book has recently appeared in English as *Richard Strauss: A Chronicle of the Early Years 1864–98* translated by M. Whittall, Cambridge University Press, Cambridge, 1982)

Notes

The most frequently quoted bibliographical sources are referred to by abbreviations, see list on previous page. For details of archive material referred to see acknowledgements on pp. 13–14.

1. *GML*.
2. *GML* and *AM*.
3. *RST Briefe*.
4. These letters are included in *GML*, pp. 376–84.
5. *AM*.
6. Ludwig Schiedermair *Musikalische Begegnungen*, Cologne, 1948, p. 46.
7. *GML*, p. 213, letter 205.
8. *AM*, p. 98.
9. *AM*, p. 51.
10. Richard Strauss, 'Grey Diary', 5, p. 12, transcribed by Alice Strauss. The 'diaries' in the Strauss-Archiv are, more properly, notebooks, in which Strauss recorded sometimes overlapping reminiscences.
11. Max Steinitzer *Richard Strauss* ninth to twelfth editions, Berlin, 1911, p. 44.
12. Quoted from Kurt Blaukopf *Gustav Mahler. Sein Leben, sein Werk und seine Welt in zeitgenössischen Bildern und Texten*, Vienna, 1976, p. 169 (published in English as *Gustav Mahler. A Documentary Study*, London, 1976).
13. Hans von Bülow, Richard Strauss *Briefwechsel* edited by Willi Schuh and Franz Trenner in *Richard Strauss Jahrbuch 1954*, Bonn, 1953, p. 54.
14. Ibid., p. 59.
15. Ibid., pp. 60f.
16. Richard Strauss, 'Blue Diary', 4, p. 25, transcribed by Alice Strauss.
17. *GML*, p. 139, letter 99.
18. Knud Martner and Robert Becqué *Zwölf Unbekannte Briefe an Ludwig Strecker (Archiv für Musikwissenschaft*, Vol. 34, No. 4), Wiesbaden, 1979.
19. Constantin Floros *Gustav Mahler, I. Die geistige Welt Gustav Mahlers in systematischer Darstellung*, Wiesbaden, 1977.
20. *GML*, p. 172, letter 149.

Notes

21 *Schuh*, p. 142.
22 Natalie Bauer-Lechner *Recollections of Gustav Mahler* (first published as *Erinnerungen an Gustav Mahler*, Vienna, 1923) edited and annotated by Peter Franklin, London, 1980, p. 30.
23 Ibid., pp. 37–8.
24 *RST Betrachtungen*, p. 168.
25 *RST Eltern*, p. 193.
26 Autographen-Auktionskatalog No. 580 (1967) by J. A. Stargardt, Marburg, quoted from *Schuh*, p. 372.
27 *Schuh*, p. 349.
28 Autograph in the Liszt Ferenc Zeneakadamia, Budapest.
29 *RST Betrachtungen*, p. 141.
30 See, for example, Theodor Reik *The Haunting Melody*, New York, 1953. The quotation is from the fifth movement of the Second Symphony.
31 Autograph in the Gustav Mahler/Alfred Rosé Room, University of Western Ontario.
32 Postcard to Arnold Berliner; autograph in the Bayerische Staatsbibliothek, Munich.
33 Ernst Otto Nodnagel *Jenseits von Wagner und Liszt*, Königsberg, 1902, p. 3.
34 Wilhelm Kienzl *Meine Lebenswanderung*, Stuttgart, 1926, p. 143.
35 *RST Betrachtungen*, p. 175; the quotation is from Erich Reinhardt's review of Mahler's Second Symphony in the *Allgemeine Musikzeitung* No. 10, 8 March 1895, pp. 139–40.
36 Letter of 14 October 1900, transcribed by Alice Strauss.
37 Ludwig Schiedermair *Musikalische Begegnungen*, Cologne, 1948, pp. 43f.
38 Bernard Scharlitt 'Gespräch mit Mahler', *Musikblätter des Anbruch*, Vol. 2, 1920, Nos. 7–8, p. 310.
39 J. B. Foerster 'Gustav Mahler in Hamburg', *Prager Presse*, 16 April 1922.
40 *GML*, p. 202, letter 190.
41 *GML*, pp. 212–4, letter 205.
42 *RST Eltern*, p. 204.
43 Ibid., p. 245.
44 Max Steinitzer *Richard Strauss*, ninth to twelfth editions, Berlin, 1911, p. 155.
45 Bruno Walter *Thema und Variationen. Erinnerungen und Gedanken*, Frankfurt, 1960, p. 217.
46 Letter to Richard Sternfeld, 10 October 1901, *RST Briefe*, p. 139.
47 Natalie Bauer-Lechner *Recollections of Gustav Mahler* (see Note 20 above), pp. 184–5.
48 Ludwig Schiedermair *Gustav Mahler*, Leipzig, 1900, pp. 13f.
49 *AM*, pp. 217–8.
50 *GML*, p. 179, letter 158.
51 *RST Eltern*, p. 251.

Notes

52 *AM*, pp. 27–8.
53 *AM*, p. 27.
54 These and the following marginal notes by Strauss on *AM* are taken from the copy of the book in the Strauss-Archiv, Garmisch-Partenkirchen, to which Alice Strauss has transferred Strauss's handwritten comments; the original is owned by Willi Schuh, Zurich.
55 *AM*, p. 28.
56 *AM*, pp. 220–1.
57 *AM*, p. 282.
58 *AM*, p. 41.
59 Letter of 31 October 1903, autograph in the Stadt- und Universitätsbibliothek, Frankfurt.
60 Letter manuscript in the Staatsarchiv, Leipzig (C. F. Peters, box 264).
61 *AM*, p. 249.
62 *AM*, p. 85.
63 Review by Romain Rolland which originally appeared in the *Revue de Paris*, 1 July 1905, and was reprinted in *Musiker von heute*, Munich, 1925, p. 237.
64 Ibid., p. 249.
65 Ibid., p. 246.
66 Letter of 5 July 1905, quoted by *Schuh*, p. 154.
67 Letter of 29 June 1903 in *Richard Strauss Autographe in München und Wien*, edited by Günter Brosche and Karl Dachs, Tutzing, 1979, p. 351.
68 *AM*, p. 260.
69 *AM*, pp. 88–9.
70 Memorandum from the General Intendant of the Royal Court Theatre to Mahler, 18 November 1901, now in the Haus-, Hof- und Staatsarchiv, Hof-Operntheater, No. 750/1901.
71 See Kurt Blaukopf *Mahler. Sein Leben* ... (see Note 12 above), p. 246.
72 Richard Specht *Gustav Mahler*, Berlin and Leipzig, 1913, p. 149.
73 *AM*, pp. 266–7.
74 *AM*, pp. 97–8 and Note on p. 363.
75 *RST Eltern*, p. 266.
76 *AM*, p. 98.
77 Klaus Pringsheim 'Zur Aufführung von Mahlers Sechster Symphonie', *Musikblätter des Anbruch*, Vol. 2, 1920, No. 14, p. 497.
78 Klaus Pringsheim 'Erinnerungen an Gustav Mahler', *Neue Zürcher Zeitung*, 7 July 1960.
79 *AM*, pp. 99–101.
80 *AM*, p. 100–1.
81 *AM*, p. 267.
82 *AM*, p. 275.
83 *AM*, p. 277.

Notes

84 Letter of 25 January 1904 quoted by Hans-Martin Plesske in 'Der Bestand Musikverlag C. F. Peters im Staatsarchiv Leipzig', *Jahrbuch der Deutschen Bücherei*, Vol. 6, 1970.
85 Letter of 14 June 1904; transcript in the Strauss-Archiv, Garmisch-Partenkirchen.
86 Letter of 21 April to Friedrich Sieger, Committee of the Frankfurt Museum Concerts, *RST Briefe*, p. 167.
87 Letter of 15 August 1906, *RST Briefe*, p. 171.
88 Friedrich von Schuch *Richard Strauss, Ernst von Schuch und Dresdens Oper*, Dresden, [1955], p. 95.
89 Letter of August 1906 from Salzburg to Alma Mahler. This appears in the original German edition only of Alma Mahler's *Gustav Mahler. Erinnerungen und Briefe*, p. 360 (see list of main bibliographical sources on p. 159).
90 *AM*, p. 276.
91 Bernard Scharlitt 'Gespräch mit Mahler' (see Note 38 above), p. 310.
92 *AM*, pp. 281–2.
93 *AM*, p. 284.
94 *AM*, p. 285.
95 *AM*, p. 286.
96 *AM*, p. 282.
97 *AM*, pp. 284–5.
98 *GML*, pp. 348–9, letter 408.
99 Richard Strauss, 'Blue Diary', 5, p. 5, transcribed by Alice Strauss.
100 *AM*, pp. 168–9.
101 Letter of February 1910 to Emil Hertzka, *Neue Zeitschrift für Musik*, Vol. 135 (1974), No. 9, p. 545.
102 *Gustav Mahler. Ein Bild seiner Persönlichkeit in Widmungen*, Munich, 1910, p. 66.
103 Richard Strauss, Diary May 1911, transcribed by Alice Strauss.
104 *RST Briefe*, p. 348.
105 Autograph in the Alma Mahler-Werfel Bequest, University of Pennsylvania.
106 *AM*, p. xli.
107 Letter of 10 October 1946, *RST Briefe*, pp. 455f.

Chronologies

compiled by Knud Martner

MAHLER CONDUCTS STRAUSS

Also sprach Zarathustra Op. 30
   New York 1, 4 and 10 November 1910

Aus Italien Op. 16
   Vienna 19 November 1899

Don Juan Op. 20
   New York 3 and 4 February 1910
   Brooklyn 11 February 1910

Feuersnot (complete opera)
   Vienna 29 January and 4 and 7 February 1902; 5 June 1905

Guntram Preludes to Acts I and II
   Hamburg 4 February 1895 (Act I only)
   Vienna 19 February 1899
   New York 30 March 1910

Ein Heldenleben Op. 40
   New York 17 and 20 January 1911

Hymnus Op. 33 No. 3 (voice and orchestra)
   Munich 8 November 1906
   St Petersburg 26 October 1907
   New York 3 and 4 February 1910
   Brooklyn 11 February 1910

Pilgers Morgenlied Op. 33 No. 4 (voice and orchestra)
   New York 7 and 10 February 1911
   Brooklyn 12 February 1911

Symphonia domestica Op. 53
   Vienna 23 November 1904

Till Eulenspiegel Op. 28
   New York 3 and 5 November and 12 December 1909
   Brooklyn 8 January 1910
   Philadelphia 17 January 1910
   New Haven 23 February 1910
   Springfield 24 February 1910
   Providence 25 February 1910
   Boston 26 February 1910
   New York 30 March 1910
   Rome 28 April 1910

Tod und Verklärung Op. 24
   New York 10 and 11 March 1910

STRAUSS CONDUCTS MAHLER (until 1911)

Symphony No. I
   Weimar ?June 1904
   Berlin 3 December 1909

Symphony No. IV
   Berlin 19 January 1909

Lieder eines fahrenden Gesellen
   Prague 14 March 1901

Three songs from *Des Knaben Wunderhorn* ('Rheinlegendchen', 'Verlor'ne Müh'', and 'Wo die schönen Trompeten')
   Berlin 9 April 1900

General Index

Adler, Guido, 150
Ahna, Pauline de, *see* Strauss, Pauline
Allgemeiner Deutscher Musikverein,
    11, 22, 27, 34, 52, 55, 71, 76, 94,
    116–19, 124–6, 132, 135–6, 141,
    151
Alsatian Musical Festival, 76, 134–5

Bahr, Hermann, 145, 156
Bauer-Lechner, Natalie, 112, 126,
    129, 161
Bayer, Josef, 69
Bayerische Staatsbibliothek, Munich,
    24, 55, 161
Becqué, Robert, 160
Beethoven, 32, 41, 113, 116–17, 123,
    135, 144
Behn, Dr Hermann, 27–8, 44–5, 113
Benecke, Dr, 155
Berliner, Arnold, 161
Berlioz, Hector, 117, 123, 139
Bertram, Theodor, 52, 59
Birrenkoven, Willy, 27, 31, 33–4,
    36–7, 39
Bland, Elsa, 83
Blaukopf, Kurt, 160, 162
Blech, Leo, 147–8
Böcklin, Arnold, 109
Brahms, Johannes, 32, 110, 116–18,
    135
Brecher, Gustav, 50, 58, 60

Brioschi, Anton, 66
Bronsart von Schellenberg, Hans, 27,
    30, 35, 116
Bronsart von Schellenberg, Ingeborg,
    33
Brosche, Günter, 162
Bruckner, Anton, 75, 104, 118, 126
Bülow, Hans von, 22, 25, 30–3,
    106–8, 110, 113–17, 119, 160
Burrian, Karl, 90
Buths, Julius, 143

Charpentier, Gustave, 126, 134–5

Dachs, Karl, 162
Dalmorès, Charles, 98
Debussy, Claude, 155
Demuth, Leopold, 59, 67–8, 83
Destinn, Emmy, 62
Dostoyevsky, Fyodor, 153

Elgar, Edward, 126

Feuerbach, Anselm, 109
Floros, Constantin, 111, 160
Flothuis, Marius, 51
Förstel, Gertrude, 76, 83, 91
Foerster, Josef Bohuslav, 121, 161
Forster, Joseph, 69
Franck, César, 134
Frankfurt Museumsgesellschaft, 121
Frankfurt Stadt- und
    Universitätsbibliothek, 162

General Index

Franklin, Peter, 161
Franz Joseph I, Emperor, 83, 123
Freund, Emil, 134
Fried, Oscar, 89, 95, 139, 143
Fürstner, Adolph, 38, 40, 51, 53, 81–2, 94, 96
Furtwängler, Wilhelm, 155

Gabrilovich, Ossip, 143
Garden, Mary, 98
Gemeentemuseum, The Hague, 61
Genossenschaft deutscher Tonsetzer, Berlin, 48, 72, 76, 132–4, 144
Gesellschaft der Autoren, Komponisten und Musikverleger (AKM), Vienna, 48, 72–3, 124, 132–4
Gluck, Christoph Willibald, 38, 40
Goebbels, Josef, 155
Goethe, Johann Wolfgang von, 37, 145, 154
Graf, Max, 67
Grasberger, Franz, 159
Grossmann, Joseph, 30
Grossmann, Paul, 30
Grützmacher, Friedrich, 20
Grützmacher, Friedrich jun., 20
Grützmacher, Leopold, 20
Gutheil-Schoder, Marie, 59, 78, 87
Gutmann, Albert, 49–50

Händel, George Frederick, 158
Hase, Oskar von, 124–5
Haus-, Hof- und Staatsarchiv, Vienna, Hof-Operntheater, 65–6, 72, 84, 162
Haydn, Joseph, 113
Hellmesberger, Josef jun., 69
Hertzka, Emil, 163
Herzog, Emilie, 47
Hitler, Adolf, 155
Hoffmann, E. T. A., 111
Hofmannsthal, Hugo von, 145–6, 156
Humperdinck, Engelbert, 68, 118, 124

Jahn, Wilhelm, 123
Jettel von Ettenach, Emil, 89

Kaim, Franz, 56–7
Kienzl, Wilhelm, 119, 124, 161
Kittel, Hermine, 78, 81
Krause, Emil, 41
Kurz, Selma, 59, 81–2

Lefler, Heinrich, 66
Leipzig Staatsarchiv, 162–3
Leoncavallo, Ruggiero, 68
Lessmann, Otto, 71, 80, 118–19, 124–5
Levi, Hermann, 19, 107, 109, 123
Lipiner, Siegfried, 129
Liszt, Franz, 32, 57–8, 77, 79–80, 110, 112–13, 117–18, 136
Löwe, Ferdinand, 75–6
Löwe, Dr Theodor, 80, 92–3, 95
Luze, Karl, 66–7

Mahler, Alma, plate 7, 15, 65, 103–5, 127–33, 135–6, 140–1, 143, 146–7, 151–2, 156, 159–63; Alma Mahler-Werfel Bequest, University of Pennsylvania, 15, 100, 156, 163
Mahler, Emma, 43, 104
Mahler, Gustav/Alfred Rosé Room, University of Western Ontario, 47, 161,
Mahler, Justine, 32, 43, 62, 104, 115, 116
Mahler, Otto, 22, 35
Mann, Thomas, 142
Markus (conductor), 58
Martner, Knud, 15, 159, 160, 164–5
Mascagni, Pietro, 68, 104, 117, 138
Mayr, Richard, 81–2
Méhul, Etienne, 117
Mendelssohn, Felix, 113
Mengelberg, Willem, 92, 143, 156

168

General Index

Merz, Oskar, 45
Meyerbeer, Giacomo, 117
Michalek, Margarete, 91–2
Mihalovich, Ödön von, 115
Mikorey, Franz, 58
Mildenburg, Anna von, 81, 83
Mitchell, Donald, 159
Moser, Anton, 76, 80
Mozart, Wolfgang Amadeus, 82–3, 113, 135, 144–5
Muck, Carl, 50, 119, 145
Müller, Max, 71
Müller-Reuter, Theodor, 70–1
Musikalische Akademie, Munich, 56–7

Naumann, Otto, 75–6
Nicodé, Jean Louis, 107
Nietzsche, Friedrich, 120–1, 146, 153–4
Nikisch, Arthur, 54, 74–5, 121, 125
Nodnagel, Ernst Otto, 118, 161

Oertel, H., 46

Paderewski, Ignacy, 126
Paul, Jean, 111
Paumgartner, Bernhard, 158
Pfitzner, Hans, 126, 136
Pfohl, Ferdinand, 26
Plaichinger, Thila, 62
Plappart von Leenheer, August, 61
Plesske, Hans-Martin, 163
Pollini, Bernhard, 21, 28–9, 31–4, 36, 38, 40, 42, 114–15
Porges, Heinrich, 45
Possart, Ernst von, 65
Preuss, Arthur, 78
Pringsheim, Klaus, 141–3, 162
Puccini, Giacomo, 138

Radecke, Robert, 107

Ranke, Leopold, 153
Reinhardt, Erich, 161
Reik, Theodor, 161
Reiter, Josef, 75
Richter, Hans, 22
Ritter, Alexander, 21, 113, 116–17
Rodin, Auguste, 157
Rolland, Romain, 135, 162
Roller, Alfred, 92–3, 97, 145, 149
Rösch, Friedrich, 75–6, 81, 132–3
Rosé, Arnold, 96–7
Rosé Collection, Ernest, 50
Rosé Collection, Maria, 53, 60

Sachs, Hans, 69
Schalk, Franz, 80, 154
Scharlitt, Bernard, 121, 146, 161, 163
Scheerbart, Paul, 47
Schiedermair, Ludwig, 105, 120, 160–1
Schillings, Max von, 54–5, 76, 79, 130, 135–6, 144
Schindler, Alma *see* Mahler, Alma
Schliessmann, Hans, 64, 137
Schmedes, Erik, 80–1, 83
Schnitzler, Arthur, 145
Schoder, Marie *see* Gutheil-Schoder, Marie
Schoenberg, Arnold, 96, 149
Schopenhauer, Arthur, 105, 122, 153
Schrödter, Fritz, 80
Schuch, Ernst von, 25–6, 87, 89–90, 144, 163
Schuch, Friedrich von, 163
Schuh, Willi, 130, 158–62
Seidl, Arthur, 105, 118, 120, 122, 141, 144
Sembach, Johannes, 76, 80
Seiger, Friedrich, 144, 163
Simons, Rainer, 84–6, 90
Sittart, Josef, 41
Slezak, Leo, 81–3

General Index

Smetana, Bedrich, 25–6, 113, 117, 138
Specht, Richard, 139, 162
Spengel, Julius, 32
Spengler, Oswald, 154
Spiess (Geheimrat), 155
Stefan, Paul, 152
Steinbach, Fritz, 124
Steinitzer, Max, 107, 160–1
Sternfeld, Richard, 161
Stoll, August, 66
Strauss, Alice, 159, 160–3
Strauss, Franz Joseph (father), 22, 71, 82, 113–14, 136
Strauss, Franz (son), 13, 159
Strauss, Pauline, 39, 65, 129, 144, 147–8, 150–1
Strauss-Archiv, Garmisch-Partenkirchen, 13, 15, 85, 91, 104, 162–3
Stritzko, Josef, 133–4

Tchaikovsky, Piotr Ilyich, 117, 126, 138
Thoma, Hans, 109
Trenner, Franz, 160

Verdi, Giuseppe, 138
Vereinigung schaffender Tonkünstler, Vienna, 74, 80

Vogl, Heinrich, 46

Wagner, Cosima, 32, 116
Wagner, Richard, 21–3, 27, 31–2, 34, 36, 46, 77, 81, 105, 108, 110, 112–13, 116–17, 123, 130, 135, 147, 149, 153, 158
Wagner, Siegfried, 124
Wagner Society in Vienna, 112, 124
Walter, Bruno, 56, 125, 161
Weber, Carl Maria von, 19, 107–9, 114, 117
Weidemann, Friedrich, 76, 78–81, 83
Weinberger, Joseph, 48, 124
Weingartner, Felix von, 30, 43, 53–4, 62, 98, 125
Werfel, Franz, 156
Whittall, Mary, 159
Wilde, Oscar, 82, 85, 136–8
Wittich, Marie, 81–2, 87
Wolf Society, Hugo, 120
Wolff (administrator), 29
Wolff, Hermann, 34, 40, 42, 113, 119
Wolff, Louise (Aloysia), 74
Wolzogen, Ernst von, 52
Wüllner, Franz, 107

Zweig, Stefan, 155–6

Index of Works by Mahler

Kindertotenlieder, 80, 125, 135
klagende Lied, Das, 22, 56–8, 60–1, 72, 92, 106, 126
Lieder eines fahrenden Gesellen, 165
Lied von der Erde, Das, 158
songs, various, 23, 47, 80, 108, 124–5, 135, 154, 165
Symphony no. 1 ('Titan'), plate 8, 19, 22–3, 27, 30, 35–6, 38, 52–3, 58, 98, 109, 111, 115–16, 118–19, 126–7, 151, 155, 158, 165
Symphony no. 2, 11, 22, 38–9, 44–5, 58, 89, 95, 110–12, 116, 119–20, 125–8, 139, 143
Symphony no. 3, 47–8, 50, 52–5, 57–9, 70, 96, 100, 120, 125–7, 132, 139, 146
Symphony no. 4, plate 5, 54–5, 57–62, 65, 70, 119, 126–7, 144, 151, 154–5, 158, 165
Symphony no. 5, 74–5, 77, 135, 142
Symphony no. 6, 94–5, 125, 141, 143
Symphony no. 7, 81, 83, 99
Symphony no. 8, 145, 151–3
Symphony no. 9, 99

Edition:
Weber, Die drei Pintos, 19, 107–9, 114

Index of Works by Strauss

Alpensymphonie, Eine, op. 64, 153
Also sprach Zarathustra, op. 30, 120, 150, 164
Aus Italien, op. 16, 20, 26, 110, 112, 124, 164
Don Juan, op. 20, 22, 26, 30, 110–11, 150, 164
Elektra, op. 58, 98, 145–6, 151
Enoch Arden, op. 38, 65
Feuersnot, op. 50, plate 4, 51–3, 56–8, 60–1, 63, 65–9, 71, 73, 75–7, 79–81, 83, 124, 129–30, 132, 136, 138, 146, 164
Guntram, op. 25, 23–7, 30–7, 39–40, 44, 114, 118, 124, 129, 146, 150, 164
Heldenleben, Ein, op. 40, 49, 77–8, 122, 124, 150, 164
Macbeth, op. 23, 26, 30, 110
Rosenkavalier, Der, op. 59, 87, 97, 99, 151
Salome, op. 54, 81–94, 96–8, 131, 136, 138–41, 146, 148, 150, 154
schweigsame Frau, Die, op. 80, 155–6
songs, various, 46, 150, 164
Symphonia domestica, op. 53, plate 11, 74, 135, 165
Symphony in F minor, op. 12, 107, 110–11
Taillefer, op. 52, 92
Till Eulenspiegel, op. 26, 43, 122–3, 150, 165
Tod und Verklärung, op. 24, 22, 26, 30, 110–11, 123, 150, 165
Wind Serenade, op. 7, 106, 111

Editions:
   Gluck, Iphigenia in Tauris, 38, 40
   Berlioz, Treatise on Instrumentation, 139
Unfulfilled projects:
   Till Eulenspiegel bei den Schildbürgern, 43
   Kometentanz, 47